# HIPPIES OF THE HAIGHT

# HIPPIES
# OF THE HAIGHT

## Sherri Cavan
*San Francisco State College*

ST. LOUIS, MISSOURI | NEW CRITICS PRESS, INC. | 1972

Published simultaneously in Canada by
Clarke, Irwin & Company Limited, Toronto and Vancouver

Library of Congress Catalog Card Number: 72-146984
SBN 0-87853-003-7

*To My Son, Adam*

# Contents

# HIPPIES OF THE HAIGHT

# Part One

# THE SOCIOLOGICAL PROBLEM

The present book may be considered a study of the Hippies of the Haight. However, I am not specifically concerned with an ethnography of the Hippies or a description of the community of the Haight. Rather, I am concerned with using this example to continue the general investigation, begun by Max Weber, of the relationship between beliefs and practices.

While the problem raised by Weber is not forgotten in sociology, in contemporary sociological work we tend routinely to treat that relationship between beliefs and practices as a constant conjunction. That is, we tend to make use of the concept of "culture" in a way which assumes there is a relationship between a people's beliefs and a people's practices, and that we know, furthermore, what that relationship looks like. For Weber, however, that relationship was always in part an open question, established only after it has been demonstrated empirically. Thus, while Weber treated the seventeenth century Protestants of Germany as a collectivity, he did not assume that their culture included the religious beliefs of Calvinism and the economic practices of capitalism. Had he done so, his study of the seventeenth century

Protestants would be judged as very limited. What was the focus of Weber's interest? He paid considerable attention to religious beliefs, but little if any to scientific, political, normative, or commonsense beliefs. He paid considerable attention to market practices, but he said little about how these Protestants behaved outside the marketplace. We are not informed of their child-rearing practices, kinship practices, conduct in home life, or relationships with other Calvinists. Nor are we told, other than in passing reference, much about their relationships with non-Calvinists. In sum, we are not told how they organized any enterprise other than their economic enterprise.

All of this omitted information would have been relevant and requisite if Weber had been writing an ethnographic description of Germanic Calvinists in the seventeenth century. However, this was not the problem in the *Protestant Ethic*. Rather, Weber was concerned with the analytic properties of social action; specifically, the way religious meaning, attributed to economic practices, guided those courses of action in particular ways and not in others.

Similarly, in the present book I am concerned with the Hippies of the Haight only insofar as observations of their activities help to trace out the interconnections between a people's beliefs and their practices. I shall begin by assuming that, for the Hippies of the Haight (as for any other group of people), there is in fact a relationship between the beliefs they hold, profess, and acknowledge, and the routine practices they sanction as proper and fitting for their members. The objective of the present investigation is to specify what the relationship between these beliefs and practices may be.

# 1

## Beliefs And Practices

How can the patterned regularity recognized as the "culture" of a society be produced from the ongoing courses of practical action persons engage in as matters of *their* individual lives? How can individual persons manage their practical activities on a day-to-day basis so that the cumulative features of social structures (such as the economy or the polity) and social institutions (such as large scale organizations or collective movements) can be observed? Flesh and blood people, who populate material social worlds, do not see themselves "acting as part of the labor force of large scale organizations." Rather, they work in factories or in corporations. They do not go about "distributing their leisure time between active and passive activities." They play golf and go to football games. They do not "inculcate the values of their group into its members." They teach others, or show them as a by-product of other activities, what is right and wrong, what is good and bad, what is beautiful and what is ugly. In short, they lead lives that they or others like them understand as proper and fitting for the time and place.[1] From a summation of the collectivity of such lives, regular, routine, and recognizable patterns of social action—

such as social structures, social institutions, normative properties, and ideological perspectives—emerge. But from the standpoint of any given person in that collectivity, life is not the flow of regular and recurrent courses of action that characterize the collectivity. Rather, it is the flux of activities, objects, and events (past, present, and potential) around a person in which he must make innumerable decisions.[2] When sociologists assume that there is a "social system" which is the structure that channels and coordinates the actions of members, they are suggesting that individuals must somehow make specific choices to act that are similar to or fit in with the choices for action made by others.[3] As individuals manage to do this satisfactorily, their conduct makes the properties of the culture that they are assumed to possess and demonstrate visible to the sociologist.

While sociologists may make abstractions of the structure of social life, the observable properties of a culture rest upon the actual behavior of individual members, each making similar decisions with respect to his own conduct.

## SPECIFICATION OF THE PROBLEM

Let us consider, as a general formulation, that individual members manage to collectively coordinate their everyday affairs through sharing a common body of social knowledge.[4]

This general framework is found in Durkheim's formulation of "collective representations;"[5] Mead's formulation of "the generalized other;"[6] and Miller, Galanter, and Pribram's formulation of "images."[7] For Durkheim, the "collective representation" sociologically conceptualized the body of social knowledge persons shared by virtue of the membership they held in particular social groups. For Mead, the "generalized other" was the body of social knowledge employed in the process of taking the role of the other. For Miller, et al., the "image" is the projected state of affairs persons hold as the anticipated consequent of their plans for practical action. Thus, whether the theoretical perspective taken is that of collective action, symbolic interaction, or individual action, matters of "social knowledge" conceptually provide flesh and blood persons with a variable resource in the management of their practical affairs.

Of this general formulation, two more specific questions may be asked: (1) What is the nature of this body of social knowledge that members share in common?; and (2) How is it employed by members as they go about their practical affairs?

The first question addresses the problem of how we are sociologically to conceptualize those matters of *social knowledge* so that the function required of the variable can be satisfied.[8] "Social knowledge" in this function is not *everything* that members know; for this would be so general as to be useless sociologically. But if it is only some part of what members know, what part?

The second question addresses the problem of how we are sociologically to conceptualize the process whereby the behavior of members, using their social knowledge, results in the actual coordination of their collective endeavor. If a body of social knowledge is employed by members as a means of coordinating (either directly or ultimately) their conduct, how is this managed? [9]

These two questions provide the specific focus of the present study of the Hippies of the Haight. My objective is not what can be learned about the Hippies by analyzing their conduct in terms of this general theoretical formulation, but, reversing that, what can be learned about the theoretical formulation by analyzing their conduct.

Thus, I have begun with the most general formulation: that it is in the common sharing of some body of *social knowledge* that members collectively coordinate their *practical affairs.* As the empirical referent of *social knowledge,* I have chosen to address the ideological beliefs that members of a group hold, profess, and acknowledge as true.[10] The basis of this choice was rather direct: an assumption that persons do in fact believe what they claim to believe. Thus, the voluntary assertions that persons make about their beliefs meet the requirement for valid measures of the variable "social knowledge." [11]

As the empirical referent of *practical affairs,* I have chosen the routine social practices members collectively engage in and collectively sanction as proper and fitting. The basis for this choice rests on the conceptual requirement that the relevant property of the practical actions undertaken by members be its manifestly co-ordinated character.[12] The coordinated patterns of collective action make the patterns of culture associated with the group demon-strable; thus the actions taken by persons which will fit within this conceptualization are those that are collectively regarded as proper and fitting.[13]

I have employed the concept *member* as the basic unit of analysis. A *member* is any person who professes a belief in the ideology commonly associated with the social group of which he is a member; and who employs that ideology as a justification for his own action or as a means of evaluating the action of others.[14] Thus, *members* are identified by the particular relationship they have to the ideology associated with some social group: they believe it and they act with respect to it. In the present study, *members* are persons who proclaim the ideology associated with "the Hippies" as true beliefs and who invoke that ideology in assessing their own conduct and the conduct of others.

The empirical problem is to investigate, within the Hippie community, how persons ideologically understand the world about them; and how persons conduct themselves socially in the course of their everyday lives.

## OVERVIEW

As co-participants in the collective life of their group, mem-bers are persons who can generally be trusted by one another in any social situation usually occurring in the life of that group.[15] This trust is established and warranted insofar as persons demonstrate their ability to know what is required of them *as members* in the present situation; and show their desire to fit into that situation in a sanctioned way. However, a member is ordinarily required to do more than merely "fit into" the ongoing situation unobtrusively.[16] He is also required to take an active part in the production of that situation as an ongoing social occasion.[17] Thus, regardless of what he may know of the social properties of *similar* kinds of situations, the practical features of the unfolding present [18] are matters that he must be able to comprehend in some sensible way and meet in some sanctioned manner. Furthermore, not only must he be able to take the social situation for granted; he must, too, be able to take his modification procedure for granted. As a member, he must be one who can keep the action of the occasion going without any systematic effort: he must keep the action going "as normal" and "normally." Only insofar as members normally keep the social action of the group going-as-normal can the cultural patterns of conduct be generated in a regular and recurrent fashion. This is the way in which unquestioned and matter-of-fact forms of everyday life take place.

Yet, unlike the players of a game, the members of a group rarely have an explicit formulation of the rules they are to follow in the normal situations of everyday life.[19] What members share in common are a set of "general understandings" about their world, and these "general understandings" in turn set the members' perceived requirements for their sanctioned practices.[20] What members know about the world-in-general does not, in this sense, define any *specific* practice members are to undertake in the course of their day. Rather, members' general understandings about the world are commonly held (and routinely employed by persons who hold them) as a *frame of reference,* to which any particular course of action can be referred so that it may be defined in a way sanctionable for the group. What members of a group routinely choose to do in the process of realizing whatever purposes, interests, or goals they may have is thus dependent upon their mutually shared knowledge of what possible choices exist.

However, since choices are not defined for any given member by a listing of a set of rules which he may point to, to specify the sanctioned status of his action, then, if members are to coordinate their action, they must *infer* the rules which they will subsequently follow, to define these choices.

The general understanding about the world that members share may in this sense be characterized as a system of cultural coordinates, *in terms of which* members attribute "social meaning" to any particular course of action they or others will or have undertaken.

The form of this process can be suggested in the following way. The language of a group may be considered the nomenclature used by the members to fix the position of an observed unit of human conduct in their cultural picture of the world.

When he is given some unit of human conduct—some bit of behavior—to examine, a member may initially "define its social meaning" by referring it to the ideological nomenclature of activities he knows—the language of objects and events that the group employs. Members can then "place" the bits of behavior in question [21] with reference to a corresponding cultural system of order. The "cultural system of order" includes the general knowledge that members have of all the following: who has the right to engage in such action, possess such objects, be present at such occasions; who has the obligation to undertake such action, deal with such objects, be responsible for such occasions. And members' knowledge of the temporal order associated with matters of activity, matters of rights, matters of obligations, components of objects, events, and practices—their characteristic features or properties—is included in the reference system used to understand some bit of behavior. Finally, this knowledge also includes the likely justifications and explanations for objects, activities, and events; and the likely consequences which follow from them.[22]

For example, for the Hippies to call (or name) some person a "straight" is to fix the position of that person as a particular social type that populates the world as it is known to the Hippies of the Haight. (For any given Hippie, the types of social persons he is likely to encounter—as a Hippie—include other "Hippies," "straights," "cool people," "tourists," teenyboppers," and "plastic Hippies." There are also "beautiful people," but this tends to be used as an abstract rather than a concrete type. As a simultaneous member of the more Orthodox American culture, he may also encounter such conventional types as "parents," "employers," "police," and "shopkeepers." However, our concern here is only with those types of persons whom he encounters while acting in the capacity of Hippie, i.e., those types of persons specific to the nomenclature of the Hippie community.)

In this sense, for a Hippie as a member of a particular social group to call someone a "straight" invokes his general cultural understandings of where "straights" fit into his picture of the world: what he can expect from them and how he is to evaluate them. Similarly, each other type of person that makes up the system of social positions that characterize the Hippie community suggests a system of relevant cultural understandings, placing members of that type into the social context.[23]

For the members of any group, then, providing the appropriate cultural name for some object, activity, or event is to locate that object, activity, or event as a part of the world as members of that group know it. At the same time, the practical significance of such objects, activities, and events are locatable by members as a matter of cultural inference. In knowing where some object, activity, or event "fits" into their picture of the world, members concomitantly know what other objects, activities, or events are relevant, as well as how they are specifically relevant in the present situation.[24]

These general understandings of the cultural order shared by members *refer* to common experiences that persons share as members of a given group. But it is not merely that, insofar as persons share common experiences, they share a common knowledge of cultural order. The social meaning of those experiences— that which makes them the same for each individual and hence common for the collectivity—presupposes a common scheme that individuals must refer to in order to *define the meaning* of those experiences.

In this way, the ideological beliefs that members hold in common about the world as both fundamental and true matters, serve as a kind of reference system that makes sense of varied individual experiences in the world.[25] What members know in common and in general about their world is from the onset ideologically refined and defined. What they may be reasonably led to expect concerning their world is not necessarily spelled out in unambiguous detail by the ideological beliefs they hold. Rather, these ideological beliefs provide them with a way of seeing, and hence understanding the world so that reasonable expectations may then be formulated by the members themselves. Thus, members applying the same ideological perspective to the same set of events should be led to the same conclusions concerning the social practices that will be sanctioned by that group.

## NOTES

1. For an extensive discussion of the perceived "rightness" of patterns of conduct, see Roger Barker and Herbert Wright, *Midwest and Its Children* (Evanston, Ill.: Row, Peterson and Co., 1955).

2. The general unfolding of social life on an everyday basis has been the primary concern of both Ernst Cassirer, *The Philosophy of Symbolic Form*, 3 Vols. (New Haven, Conn.: Yale University Press, 1965), and Alfred Schutz, *Collected Papers*, 3 Vols. (The Hague: Martinus Nijhoff, 1964, 1966).

3. "Cultural Anthropology and Linguistics," in Dell Hymes, ed., *Language in Culture and Society* (New York: Harper and Row, 1964), p. 36. Emphasis added. Similar statements can be found in Alfred Schutz, *Collected Papers*, Vol. I (The Hague: Martinus Nijhoff, 1962), pp. 27–47, and Max Weber, *The Methodology of the Social Sciences* (New York: The Free Press, 1949).

4. Peter Berger and Thomas Luckman, *The Social Construction of Reality* (Garden City, N.Y.: Doubleday and Co., 1966), pp. 45–118.

5. Emile Durkheim, *The Elementary Forms of Religious Life* (Glencoe, Ill.: The Free Press, n.d.).

6. George H. Mead, *Mind, Self and Society* (Chicago: University of Chicago Press, 1934).

7. George A. Miller, Eugene Galanter, and Karl Pribram, *Plans and the Structure of Behavior* (New York: Holt, Rinehart, and Winston, 1960), as well as Gilbert Ryle, *The Concept of Mind* (New York: Barnes and Noble, 1965), pp. 25–61.

8. Insofar as the substantive information that "social knowledge" contains is assumed to vary from group to group, the theoretical role which the concept takes is that of a variable.

9. This problem faced by the members of a group or society is one of living in accordance with the cultural conventions. For example, Morris Opler writes with respect to the Chiricahua Apaches' cultural themes of male superiority that there are occasions where women's behavior is formally specified in ceremonial events. But there are also what Opler has called "unformalized expressions" of the theme:

> "The actual expression of the theme, consequently, becomes a function of a web of elements and therefore, cannot be agreed upon in advance. What is really expected of the woman is that she meet any novel or unexpected situation in which men are involved in the spirit of the theme. As far as specific behavior is concerned, she is allowed various solutions compatible with a socially accepted standard of conduct."

"Themes as Dynamic Forces in Culture," *AJS*, Vol. 51 (1946), p. 200. See also Harold Garfinkel, *Studies in Ethnomethodology* (Englewood Cliffs, N.J.: Prentice-Hall, 1967), Egon Bittner, "Police Discretion in Emergency Apprehension of Mentally Ill Persons," *Social Problems*, Vol. 14 (1967), pp. 278–292, and David Mandelbaum, "From Variation and Meaning of a Ceremony," in Robert Spencer, ed., *Method and Perspective in Anthropology* (Minneapolis, Minn.: University of Minnesota Press, 1964), pp. 60–102.

10. Malinowski's concern with the adequacy of his formulation of the Trobriand belief system on the basis of *both* members' assertions about what they believe and members' practices seems to reflect just this problem. See *Magic, Science and Religion* (Garden City, N.Y.: Doubleday Anchor, 1955), pp. 241–244. Also relevant is Irwin Deutscher's discussion in "Words and Deeds," *Social Problems*, Vol. 13 (1966), pp. 235–254.

11. The problem of reliability is a strictly methodological problem, and was solved by treating as "Hippie beliefs" those ideological assertions that were general in the community at large.

12. By "sanctioned practices," I shall mean any course of action undertaken which is treated as a proper and fitting course of action on the part of other members. For a practice to be "unsanctioned," it must in effect be censured by other members. For a full explication of this use, see Emile Durkheim, *The Division of Labor in Society* (Glencoe, Ill.: The Free Press, 1960), pp. 411–435.

13. Thus, I shall not be concerned with how members come to transgress rules, but how they manage to comply with them.

14. See, for example, Harold Garfinkel's use of the term "member" in *Proceedings of the Purdue Symposium on Ethnomethodology,* Richard Hill and Kathleen Crittenden, eds. (Purdue University: Institute for the Study of Social Change, 1968).

15. See Harold Garfinkel, "A Conception of and Experiments with 'Trust' as a Condition of Stable Concerted Actions," in O. J. Harvey, ed., *Motivation and Social Interaction* (New York: The Ronald Press, 1963), pp. 187–238.

16. Cf. Barker and Wright, *op. cit.,* pp. 84–109.

17. Cf. Erving Goffman, *Behavior in Public Places* (London: Collier-Macmillan, 1963), pp. 43–63.

18. Cf. Herbert Blumer, "Psychological Import of the Human Group," in *Group Relations at the Crossroads,* Muzafer Sherif and M. O. Wilson, eds. (New York: Harper and Brothers, 1953), pp. 185–202.

19. Harold Garfinkel's writings on ethnomethodology in a very broad sense focus on just this general problem. See *Studies in Ethnomethodology, op. cit.,* particularly pp. 1–24 and 76–115. Relevant also is Bittner, *op. cit.,* and Don Zimmerman, "The Practicalities of Rule-Use," in Harold Garfinkel, H. Sacks, and L. Churchill, eds., *Contributions to Ethnomethodology* (Bloomington, Ind.: Indiana University Press), forthcoming.

20. Cf. Anthony Wallace, *Culture and Personality* (New York: Random House, 1967), particularly pp. 1–26.

21. Cf. Clark McPhal, "Student Walkout," *Social Problems,* Vol. 16 (1969), pp. 441–445.

22. Cf. Sherri Cavan, *Liquor License* (Chicago: Aldine Publishing Co., 1966), Chap. 1.

23. Cf. Charles Frake, "How to Ask for a Drink in Subanum," *American Anthropologist,* Vol. 66, pt. 2 (1964), pp. 127–132.

24. The procedure might most aptly be described by the metaphor of "literal cultural pictures in persons' heads" in which, in focusing in on some part of an array of cultural order graphically portrayed, other relevant properties of the array are made visible. This general notion seems to be subsumed in *Explorations in Transactional Psychology*, Franklin P. Kilpatrick, ed. (New York: New York University Press, 1961).

25. This general problem is discussed by Karl Mannheim both in *Ideology and Utopia* (New York: Harcourt Brace and Co., 1936), pp. 64–70, and in *Essays on the Sociology of Knowledge* (London: Routledge and Kegan Paul, 1959), pp. 33–83.

# 2

## Methodological Procedures

The observer describes what members of a community *do* on a day-to-day basis in order to organize the diverse courses of action that are salient facts of the life of the community into a coherent whole. Standing outside of the routine activities of the life of the members, the observer takes a particular perspective on those activities. He "sees" them as interrelated parts of the "way of life" of the community. For example, he "sees" how a "typical day" is composed, even though the members themselves may, at any given time, be explicitly aware of only segments of such days. This is not to say that the observer will see something the members can never see. If at any time the members were to stop participating, and reflect back upon what they had participated in, they too would be provided with the organizing perspective utilized by the observer. In this sense, the discovery of the culture of a group ("the way things are around here; what we do") is not the discovery of the observer. Rather, it is the discovery of the reflective actor who, once removed from the immediacy of action, sees the world with a new purpose.[1] For the members of a group, the purpose of their action is eminently practical: coming to terms with their circumstances. Under such conditions, they need attend only to as much of their "life in general" as is relevant to those purposes. A member need be focally aware of only that segment that immediately concerns him.

For the observer, the purpose of observation is theoretical: making sense of those circumstances, which are now not matters of ongoing action, but matters of completed action. Under such conditions, he is free to evoke as much of the "life in general" as he thinks is relevant to answer the questions he has raised. He needs to be focally aware of only that segment of action which is of theoretical interest.

One of the most frequent criticisms made of descriptive studies in sociology is that the data are, at most, impressionistic, and hence the conclusions of such studies are a matter of conjecture. An adequate answer to this criticism is not simply to number the observed instances contained in one's field notes, allowing the number of times some particular social event appears to attest to its sociological significance. Rather, an adequate answer to such criticisms rests on a clear explication of how the evidence contained in one's descriptive notes was assessed.[2]

In the context of the present study, statements such as "I observed 127 instances of panhandling in the Haight," are irrelevant. I am not concerned with how many Hippies panhandle; or whether panhandling in the Haight is done frequently or occasionally. If I consider the phenomenon of panhandling it is because what I am concerned with is *the way the ideology Hippies proclaim serves to sanction panhandling as a course of practical action on their part.* First, what makes a phenomenon important to consider is the existence of an activity in the community on a routine basis. (For example, any walk down Haight Street is likely to result in at least one observed instance of panhandling, sometimes by different Hippies, sometimes by the same Hippies.) Second, what is important is that Hippies, who are themselves not engaged in panhandling, treat the activity as a sensible and sanctioned course of action. (For example, they give good reasons to one another for why people panhandle; they do not admonish the panhandler; and they sometimes part with some "spare change" when they are panhandled on the street.)

These two qualitatively ordered *facts*—that panhandling takes place routinely on the part of some Hippies and that it is both sensible and sanctioned by other Hippies—constitute relevant coded data. The facts *refer* to the observed incidents recorded in field notes. However, the incidents are only raw data, equivalent to the actual answers given by respondents to the questions put to them in an interview situation.

Thus, in the present chapter I would like to specify as explicitly as possible the actual procedures I have employed in the assessment of the evidence contained in the observational data, and the assumptions underlying these procedures.

In treating the recorded incidents of the Haight as "raw data," my concern has been with transforming that body of evidence into factual assertions concerning (1) the activities that routinely take place in the Haight; (2) the substantive character of those activities; and (3) whether those activities are sanctioned or censured.

This transformation can be exemplified by considering how the evidence for one kind of activity, "happenings," was assessed.

| *Recorded Information* | *Facts* |
|---|---|
| A note of October, 1969, that dances at two auditoriums take place virtually every weekend and have been occurring for over a year now. | *Happenings take place as a part of everyday life in the Haight.* |
| The knowledge (not recorded as such) that dances have taken place at two other auditoriums in the city on a number of occasions. | |
| Clippings from Underground newspapers referring to different Hippie-acknowledged "happenings" in the park and on Haight Street. | |
| Field notes describing four different observations at auditoriums. | |

Field notes describing three different observed occasions of street gatherings.

The newspaper clipping descriptions (noted above).

Seven recorded observations of conversations where the salient topic was "happenings."

A number of recorded incidents of conversations where happenings are mentioned by me as "relevant" to the occasion at hand (e.g., when a dance is the occasion for deciding to panhandle).

Notes contained in some (but not all) of the material listed above referring to how "happenings" are evaluated (e.g., group reminiscence of happenings).

*Happenings ordinarily look like this . . .*

*Happenings are generally treated like this . . .*

The facts are not "self-evident" matters. They are my judgment of the content of the incidents notes on the left. However, the judgment employed is exactly the same kind of judgment that coders of interview schedules must make when they code open-ended questions asked of some specified sample of respondents. Similarly, it is the same kind of judgment that observers of small group interaction must make when they record an exchange between the participating subjects as instances of "showing solidarity," or "showing tension release."

Thus recorded incidents supply the body of factual evidence on which the study is based. These incidents are coded in terms of:

A. Hippie beliefs about
    1. the world in general
    2. moral maxims
    3. drugs
B. The everyday practices of
    4. dressing
    5. eating
    6. working
    7. just being
    8. being social

9. happenings
10. maintaining one's body
11. maintaining one's psyche
12. maintaining one's community
13. preventing trouble
14. coping with trouble
15. explaining trouble
16. smoking grass
17. buying grass
18. laying grass
19. giving grass
20. requesting grass

It should be noted that in no way do the practices listed above constitute any definitive statement of everything members of the Hippie community of the Haight-Ashbury do on an everyday basis. They do these things and do many other things as well. The status of the practices that have been included in the present study is that they all are items that members would include in the *set of all possible sanctioned practices.*

This *set* consists of everything that one member *could* do and that would be treated by other members as a sanctioned mode of conduct. It should be clear that the *set* includes not only what Hippies have done, but what they are yet to do as well. The criteria for inclusion in the set are merely (1) that it be done by someone who also claims to be a member, and (2) it must be sanctioned by others who also claim to be members.

It must also be clear that the *set of all possible sanctioned practices* itself is not necessarily explicit for any given group. Insofar as there is no definitive listing of sanctionable practices for members of a group, at any time those who are engaged in action and those who are engaged in responding to that action can dispute the matter of appropriate judgment regarding some questionable activity. Such disputes would in effect deny that one party or the other actually accept the beliefs that claiming membership implies and actually acts on his beliefs. This criteria, however, raises certain problems with respect to the present study. Not all persons to be found in the district acknowledge the ideology as true and relevant. Furthermore, there are some persons who acknowledge the ideology as true, but not relevant to themselves. And finally, there are still others who acknowledge some parts of the ideology as true and relevant to themselves and other parts of the ideology as irrelevant and/or false.

In the incidents recorded in my field notes, I have tried wherever possible to indicate what I knew about the position of those observed with respect to the Hippie ideology. In some cases there has been no problem in assigning people to the category of "member": at one time or another, they have stated their own position explicitly. However, I have also assigned people to membership on the basis of their being acknowledged as "Hippies" by other persons whose position I knew. Furthermore, in many situations all I knew was that people were dressed like members, spoke like members, were located in places where members were routinely found, and were acting in ways quite similar to the ways members ordinarily acted. But in formulating the descriptions of sanctioned Hippie practices, I have tended to give the greatest weight to those field incidents where I was most certain of the membership status of the participants.

## METHOD OF ANALYSIS

The following chapter presents a general history of the Haight-Ashbury District (from about 1961 to about 1966). The purpose of this chapter is to provide a background for the circumstances of the Hippies of the Haight, and to indicate some of the events instrumental in the Hippie community becoming recognized as such. The history of the Haight-Ashbury District is in part the history of the Hippies of the Haight as well.

Chapter 4 focuses on the Hippie ideology: what the Hippies of the Haight believe as matters of focal awareness; how they describe what their life is all about, what its purpose is; how they explain why things must be as they believe them to be; what they proclaim as truth and accept as fact; what they demand as matters of moral conduct.

Chapters 5–8 constitute the analysis of the data. In each chapter, I have selected a particular topic for investigation. The topic of Chapter 5 is *everyday life* in the Haight: the commonplace features of the daily round, as it is defined by members. The topic of Chapter 6 is that of *social exchange:* how members obtain goods and evaluate those transactions. In Chapter 7 the topic is that of *social trouble:* the problematic features of life as they are defined by members. In Chapter 8, the topic is *social control:* how members subsequently manage the trouble they encounter.

In each chapter, I have tried to specify the particular properties these topics of social life have as they are to be observed in the Hippie community, and suggest the ideological coordinates the actual observed practices can have. Thus, in each of these chapters, the general problem is the same: given the ideology available to the members of the group as matters of their shared understandings of the world, what coordinates of this system of belief are available to members to match with their actual practices, and hence, to make sense of those practices? As a means of describing the sanctioned practices of members, I have employed the following working model: If a member does X-Y-Z in the presence of other acknowledged members and those other acknowledged members do not censure the practice, I shall assert that members consider X-Y-Z a sanctionable or socially tolerable course of action. If a member does R-N-P in the presence of other acknowledged members and the other acknowledged members do censure the practice, I shall assert that members do not consider R-N-P a sanctionable course of action. In this way, the sanctioned status of any *given* practice can be determined with respect to any particular instance that has been observed. The particular items that members would include in the *set of all-possible-sanctioned-practices* are of theoretical relevance. For it is this set of practices that has been theoretically conceptualized as activities that members perceive as ideologically justified.

The final descriptions of everyday life, of social exchange, social trouble, and social control are in effect a model constructed of empirically sanctioned practices. This model is not intended to be a definitive statement of what members of the Hippie community of the Haight-Ashbury do, but only an exemplification of some of the practices they treat as proper and fitting on the part of members.

As a final note concerning the method of analysis: the data collected during the course of the field work (as will be explained subsequently) varied in both systematic character and the range of sub-population sample. Thus, the strongest possible assertion the data will support is of the kind, "Some Hippies do *this* and other Hippies *sanction* the behavior." In such an assertion, the "this" and the "sanction" are fully specifiable in terms of the records of empirical events actually occurring in the community. The "some" and the "other" as numbers of empirical events actually occurring in the community cannot be addressed because the actual sub-populations of members observed may bias the relative frequencies of the items occurring for observation.

It can be argued that, with such a procedure, the normative emphasis placed upon the various items (whether it is mandatory, preferential, acceptable, or dubious) is not made clear. However, the evaluative ranking of the items included with the practice (e.g., whether the Hippies of the Haight consider working rather than begging a *more* acceptable means of coping with their troubles or vice versa) is not a question in the present study. Rather, what is of concern are the *various* procedures for coping that are recognized as sanctioned procedures in the community; and how these particular procedures are related to the ideological tenets proclaimed by members.

I have presented, in the body of the text, a variety of field examples of the observed items to which the practices included

in the normative model refer. The particular examples I have
chosen are those which I felt showed most clearly the relevant
feature of the particular activity in question. In the course of
data-collection, there were frequent opportunities for me to question activities from the position of participant-in-the-present-
situation. Such questions provide particularly good examples of
sanctioned practices insofar as they typically evoke specific justifications of those actions members have just taken.

## DATA COLLECTION

I moved to the Haight-Ashbury District in the summer of
1961 and have lived there continually since, with the exception of
six weeks during the summer of 1962 and six weeks during the
summer of 1967.

From 1961 to 1963 I collected occasional, non-systematic
observations, clippings, and notes on the District. In 1963 my
notes were still occasional, although I began to make more systematic observations. Around this time I joined, and became (as a
resident of the District) an active member in the Haight-Ashbury
Neighborhood Council. My membership in the Council has continued since then, although my involvement in and observations
of the activities of the Council have been more consistent at some
times than at others. Through the Council I came to know the self-
identified leaders of what came to be called "The Straight Community" in the District. Through them I later came to know the
self-identified leaders of the Hippie community. While one can
distinguish the two communities residing in the District, there is
nevertheless occasional interchange at the top of each system,
and knowing one facilitated knowing the other.

During the ongoing course of my residence in the District, I
became acquainted with about ten or twelve people who identified
themselves with the Hippie community. These were people whom
I could freely visit, unannounced, at their residences. And these
people freely came to visit me. All of them knew I was a

sociologist, but in the ongoing social life of the community that was often treated by them as irrelevant.

Like any community, the Hippie community is in some ways a unified phenomenon, but it also has its smaller segments, characterized by particular patterns of behavior that are sanctioned by the community in general, but are not general in the community.[3] These segments of the Hippie community consisted of:

1. The intensified drug scene
2. The political occasional-activists
3. The mystics
4. Those who are "simply living"
5. The intensified self-seekers
6. The Diggers
7. The Hell's Angels

I made no active attempt to "select" out acquaintances on the basis of what segment of the Hippie community they were most involved with. As it turned out, those acquaintances I did make were mainly drawn from the first four.

Through this small group I gradually made nodding acquaintance with other members of the Hippie community. In addition, the public settings of the community provided easy and normal access to meeting, talking with, and listening to members of the community in general.

When I eventually decided to study the Hippie community, I did not announce this either to the members of the community in general nor to those I knew well. However, I occasionally discussed the sociological observations and analyses I had made of the community with the latter; and I have given one or two of them papers, or parts of papers, to read and comment on. In effect, in terms of research strategy, I was neither a known nor unknown observer of the scene. I was simply there.

My observations (which extended up to 1968) covered an extensive range of regular and routine events in the Haight. They included events in the (public) streets, the shops, the coffee houses, the parks, the dances, the happenings, meetings, pads, parties, a variety of backstage regions, and a host of members' conversations with one another. Specific segments of the life which I have *not* had an opportunity to observe at length include: The Diggers (outside of the Free Store and their public activities); the Hell's Angels (outside of a few encounters in coffee shops and their activity on the street); acid trips; occasions of actual methedrine use; the Hippie life that takes place regularly outside of the Haight (in the country, at the beach, and in other parts of the country; and the insides of buses and trucks). There may be other parts of the life I have not observed directly, but since I have no indirect knowledge of them either, I cannot list them.

Since I began making observations before I actually decided to treat the community as a sociological problem, my field notes are of two kinds: systematic and non-systematic. The latter are those I made in the beginning. They cover anything that struck me as being "interesting" at the time I observed it. When I decided to be more systematic, I began to focus on the courses of action that seemed to be routine events on the part of the members. After formulating the theoretical problem I wanted to address, I realized that many of my notes already focused on matters of ideology as well as matters of activity. I had, without specific intent, simply included ideological matters as a part of "what usually happens in the Haight."

With respect to the systematic focused observations, in my attempts as an observer to "see" what the community was like, I began essentially by listening first and looking afterward, on the assumption that what members were saying *to each other* would at least tentatively direct me in how to look at their world and what they did in it in the same way they did.[4] I listened in two senses: metaphorically, by reading whatever they wrote (the Underground newspapers, the books and pamphlets, the handouts, the notices tacked on the windows and on the bulletin boards inside the shops). And I listened literally, to their conversations and verbal exchanges with one another in whatever settings and occasions I could.

I assumed that what they said to one another was comprehensible to them, regardless of whether those matters also made sense to me at that time. Given such studious naïveté on my part, I found myself in the position of generally understanding what they were talking of—the topics of conversation—but not necessarily what they were talking *about*—the meaning of those conversations.

The meaning of those conversations—as well as the activities that accompany them and exist independent of them—became the sociological question to answer: how and in what way were these *meaningful* events for the members?

Since the topics of members' conversation—and the manifest reason of their activity—were not treated as problematic, my final decision was to take the most frequent topics I observed as the main areas for the study. These were: "drugs," "making it," and "beliefs." However, it became apparent quite early in the research that, while matters categorized under the heading "beliefs" could be summarized in a general fashion, matters categorized under the other topic headings were too large, too ambiguous, and in large measure, interrelated as matters of practical action.

In the course of specifying the research into manageable terms, I divided the topic of "drugs" into two parts: "obtaining drugs," and "using drugs." The former initially included all items members referred to as drugs. This list includes marijuana, LSD-25, psilocybin, methamphetamine, mescaline, DMT, and STP as the major drugs (although references also included morning-glory seeds, woodrose seeds, nutmeg, rhododendron petals, and a few other substances). I eventually decided to focus only on obtaining marijuana, insofar as it was the most frequently obtained drug in the community, and thus the most visible for purposes of observation.

The information contained under "using drugs" included

both matters referring to members' actual drug use and matters referring to members' comments about the drug experience. Insofar as all of my notes that made reference to members' actual drug use also make reference to other social activities that took place concurrently, I have chosen to focus on "drug use" only as it was implicated in the routine course of members' everyday activity, since for many of the Hippies of the Haight, "taking drugs" is much like "drinking" for patrons of a bar,[5] both in actual practice and in stated meaning. I chose to focus on accounts of the experience of time in relation to drug experiences. For of all the drug-related experiences which the Hippies of the Haight recounted, these were the ones that seemed to have the most relevance for their collective enterprise, affecting how they coordinate the ongoing courses of their practical activities.

Once the items on the topic of "drugs" had been specified into a manageable conceptual problem, the topic of "making it" (the term Hippies used for living their lives) was respecified in terms of two general problems: How members know trouble and how members manage trouble. These topical categories—beliefs, everyday social practices, obtaining marijuana, knowing trouble, and managing trouble—thus became the "variables" that were to be analyzed.

## NOTES

1. See Alfred Schutz, *Collected Papers*, Vol. I: The Problem of Social Reality (The Hague: Martinus Wijhoff, 1962), pp. 27–47, and Harold Garfinkel, *Studies in Ethnomethodology* (Englewood Cliffs, N.J.: Prentice-Hall, 1967), pp. 262–283.

2. Cf. Aaron Cicourel, *The Social Organization of Juvenile Justice* (New York: John Wiley and Sons, 1968), Chap. 1; Sherri Cavan, *Fieldguide to Sociology,* unpublished MS.

3. For a more extended discussion of internal differentiation in the "Hippie movement" in general, in terms of what forms of activity are accentuated, see Geoffrey Simmon and Grafton Trout, "Hippies in

College—From Teeny-boppers to Drug Freaks," *trans*action, Vol. 5 (1967), pp. 27–32.

4. Cf. Susan Ervin-Tripp, *Sociolinguistics,* Working Paper #3, University of California, Berkeley, Language-Behavior Research Laboratory, Mimeo, 1967, pp. 63–68.

5. Cf. Sherri Cavan, *Liquor License* (Chicago: Aldine Publishing Co., 1966).

# Part Two

---

# THE PROBLEM
# FOR INVESTIGATION

The collectivity of persons known in sociology as a "social group," can be located by any of three analytic properties. First, they may be located in terms of the historical place they occupy in time and space.[1] It is in this sense that we may refer to the seventeenth century Protestants as a "group" of people. Second, they may be located in terms of a commonly shared system of beliefs. It is in this sense that we may refer to Calvinists as a "group" of persons. Finally, they may be located in terms of their practices. In this sense we may refer to Capitalists as a "group" of persons.

These analytic properties, taken concurrently, specify that empirical domain of phenomena we define as "culture." "Culture" is not the property of an unspecified collectivity of individual persons, but rather the unique property of a particular social group.[2] In this sense, we can specify a particular group of persons as a sociological means of pointing to the empirical location of a particular culture. Thus, in pointing to the empirical location of the Protestant culture, the social group which was of interest to Weber, for example, was composed of seventeenth century Germanic peoples who were as well Calvinists and Capitalists.

As an empirical social group, the Hippies of the Haight constitute a unique historical event, just as seventeenth century Protestants were a unique historical event. Thus, as a matter of specifying the collectivity of persons to be studied, the Hippies of the Haight are in no way to be thought of as a random cross section of America. Nor are they persons who are all engaged in some common identifiable activity, other than "being Hippies" (as all persons receiving welfare checks; all persons employed in some particular organization or in some particular capacity in an organization; all persons with an arrest record, or the like). But they can be located as a unique historical event, either in terms of their location, their ideological beliefs, or their social practices. In the present section I shall specify membership in that group through two analytic properties: the particular territory in which those persons can be found; and the system of beliefs they proclaim.

As flesh and blood persons, the Hippies of the Haight were found living out their everyday life in the ecological confines of the Haight-Ashbury District and making sense of their own lives, and the lives of others in the District, in terms of the Hippie creed. They recognized each other in the same way they recognized themselves as Hippies. Thus for any given bona-fide member, any other he recognizes as "a Hippie" could be taken to be a member also. In this way, a collectivity of Hippies could be recognized (empirically measured). One need only know the identity of one Hippie, where he lives his life, and what he believes about his life. As the initial member, his considered judgments of associates could be taken to validate the status of those others: as fellow members, or others, such as Plastic Hippies, Teenyboppers, Tourist, Straight, and Cool.[3] Once any additional given member has been recognized, he too can be considered a bona-fide (valid) member of the empirical community in question. And hence, the subsequent recognition of membership on the part of these bona-fide members serve empirically to validate the membership of still others. The logic of the sampling procedure is, of course, exactly the same as used in both the reputational and "snow-balling" sample techniques.

As a practical research feature, then, it was only necessary to have known one bona-fide Hippie to ascertain the identity of any array of persons in the District for consideration as bona-fide members as well. Further, on the basis of the regularity of distribution of known Hippies into definable subparts of the setting,[4] identification was made of typical or usual Hippie locales in the District: places where bona-fide members routinely congregated. As a sampling procedure, it was assumed that anyone who apparently "fit in" to the situation could be taken to be a bona-fide member, unless evidence was presented to the contrary. For instance, if one person who apparently "fit in" made an issue of the status of another (e.g., pointed him out as a tourist) and others who also apparently "fit in" seemed to find this view tolerable (e.g., offered no noticeable censure). Any confidence in the validity of the following empirical assertions must be understood in terms of this procedure that was employed in the process of data collection.

# NOTES

1. Nelson Goodman, *The Structure of Appearance* (Indianapolis, Ind.: The Bobbs-Merrill Co., 1966).

2. Emile Durkheim, *Elementary Forms of Religious Life* (Glencoe, Ill.: The Free Press, n.d.).

3. These are the specific social types which are routinely recognized by members of the Hippie community on a day-to-day basis.

4. Cf. Roger Barker and Herbert Wright, *Midwest and Its Children* (Evanston, Ill.: Row, Peterson & Co., 1955), pp. 45–83.

# 3

## The Hippies in the Haight

One way the members of any social group can be located is in terms of the historical place they occupy in time and space. In this sense, the "Hippies" shall be defined as a "collectivity of identical individuals living in the Haight-Ashbury District between 1966 and 1968." This is a methodological definition, specifying certain persons who are to be subject to further study. The individual persons are to be considered "identical" in that they share in common some defining attribute of the class; and hence, taken individually, they are to be considered as identical instances of that class.[1] In this way, the sociological conceptualization of "the Hippies" shall refer to flesh and blood persons, who can be seen and whose actions can be recorded.

### SOCIAL TOPOGRAPHY OF THE HAIGHT

The Haight-Ashbury District is almost in the geographic center of San Francisco. In the view of San Franciscans, it is not notable for being either in what they call "the warm belt" or in what they call "the fog belt." The usual climate includes some sunshine and some heavy fog. The District is bounded on the west by Golden Gate Park, on the south by the far slope of the hilly area, called either Buena Vista or Ashbury Heights or Upper Terrace. For the Haight-Ashbury Neighborhood Council, the eastern boundary of the District is Divisidero Street; the northern boundary of the District is Fulton Street. The City Planning Commission sometimes uses these streets in the definition of the District; sometimes streets a few blocks away.

The terrain of the District is variable. About half of it is relatively level ground, and is called by the old residents "The Flats." The rest of the area is covered with hills of varying steepness. This area is called "The Hill," or sometimes "The Heights."

Within the boundaries there are two separate parks. The Panhandle is a block wide and four blocks long. It contains a wide strip of grass, asphalt paths, and eucalyptus trees. When Golden Gate Park was first developed, this strip was the carriage entrance to the park. The second park, Buena Vista, is also quite large. It is a natural hill park, where the paths are mostly gravel and dirt and where blackberries grow wild in the summer. From the top of Buena Vista one can see the entire city, this panorama includes the Oakland Bay Bridge and the Golden Gate Bridge.

Each park contains a small children's playground. In addition, there are tennis courts in Buena Vista and a basketball court in the Panhandle.

The main thoroughfare in the District is Haight Street. Haight Street begins at Market Street, just beyond the downtown section, and ends at a pedestrian entrance into Golden Gate Park. The last five blocks of Haight Street are a neighborhood-oriented commercial enclave. There are two elementary schools in the District, one parochial school, one high school, and five churches (as well as a varying number of storefront churches). Other institutions include a branch library, a football stadium, a boys' club, and two hospitals. Less immediately visible is a home for unwed mothers and a resident boardinghouse for non-institutionalized mental retardates. The University of California Medical Center is adjacent to the western boundary of the District, the University of San Francisco faces the northern boundary, and a third hospital is just across the street which marks the eastern boundary. Two main traffic thoroughfares go through the northern part of the District, leading directly toward and away from the Freeway and the Bay Bridge approach.

For many of the residents, this list describes what the District has "always" contained. This array of urban facilities was what was physically there when the Hippies came. However, what the District contained socially when the Hippies arrived is very significant. The Haight-Ashbury has been a self-conscious community for many years. Those who have lived here a score or more years, talk nostalgically about the early Forties, when the activists in the labor unions made the District their home. The old residents in general see the Haight-Ashbury as having always been a "working class residential district with a liberal and progressive atmosphere." They still talk with self-conscious pride of the fact that the District has been considered by themselves and others as well as one of San Francisco's first successfully integrated neighborhoods, both in terms of race and economic and social position.[2]

In the late Fifties and early Sixties, changes in the District occurred. Redevelopment and relocation activity in the adjacent ghetto areas resulted in a large influx of Blacks, primarily into the less expensive residences in "The Flats." The self-conscious liberal tradition on the part of the most vocal group of current residents made "not making an issue of the influx" a major issue. The Haight-Ashbury Neighborhood Council (which began in 1960) treated as one of its main goals the maintenance of racial and economic integration in the District.

About this same time, the openly proclaimed "liberal atmosphere" of the residents provided an effective milieu for the development and maintenance of radical political groups. The Neighborhood Council sponsored a SNCC worker to help organize the Black poor in the area. Such sponsorship was provided even though the Council members themselves felt at the time that such organizations of the disenfranchised might be contrary to the vested interests of the franchised residents. Somewhat later, for a period of better than a year, the Haight-Ashbury Vietnam Day Committee became a vocal and visible group in the area. Again in a highly self-conscious fashion, the residents of the District saw themselves as "liberal" (if not necessarily "radical") and they seemed determined not to shirk the implications that their commitment to that definition generated. Merged in with the "liberal tradition" was a "bohemian tradition." For many years there had been a number of writers, artists, and actors living in the District. However, this element was not distinguished in any particularly notable way; they were simply there as a part of the District in general.

With the gradual dissolution of the North Beach "beat scene" in the late Fifties and early Sixties, many of the residents from the Beach moved to the Haight-Ashbury.[3] By 1964, the old residents saw the Haight-Ashbury as a district which was, as a composite, "a liberal, sometimes radical, successfully integrated, bohemian, working class, residential area."

What for some reason seems to be "forgotten" on the part of the old residents is that, in mid-1964, the Haight-Ashbury was also, in part at least, a district for deviants as well. By "forgotten" I mean that I literally never heard the fact mentioned in the conversations of old residents about the pre-Hippie history of the District. When I would remind them, they would typically look at me with an uncertain expression and say, "Oh, I forgot about that."

In the early part of 1964 (allegedly because of the moderately priced Victorian houses which could be elegantly restored) there was a substantial influx of homosexual bars in the District and areas immediately adjacent to it. In the homosexual community of San Francisco, both Haight Street and the nearby parks became known as excellent areas for "cruising."

I am uncertain from my observations during that period whether it was the case that the old residents "saw" the homosexuals but chose to ignore them, or whether it was the case that they did not "see" the homosexuals because it was outside the kind of general knowledge they had about their world. While the former seems likely in terms of the old residents' self-conscious liberality, the latter seems likely in terms of the way the homosexual influx was finally resolved.

There had been for many years a neighborhood movie theater on Haight Street. In 1963 the theater closed, presumably for economic reasons. Although many of the residents at the time voiced concern and interest in having it reopened, it remained closed until the early summer of 1964. At that time it was reopened and redecorated inside with paintings of semi-nude males. The marquee proclaimed the showing of "gay" films.[4] The immediate response of the residents, as voiced through the Neighborhood Council, the PTA's, and various gatherings of unaffiliated residents, was indignation and then outrage. The theater stood, as they saw it, as a clear sign of the "ruin" of the neighborhood (although nothing was said either about the gay bars or the homosexuals living in the area).

The conclusion of this era of the District can be most easily described by the main article of the District newspaper which, like the District itself, had up to this time been consistently and self-consciously "liberal."

### GAY HAIGHT SHOW CLOSED: OWNERS FLEE

An eastern gangster syndicate discovered that the Haight-Ashbury neighborhood was tougher than they bargained for.

The nation's first and only homosexual movie house was closed after only one month in operation.

The owners blew town in a new convertible with two female impersonators in the back seat. The police are on their tail for jumping bail and writing a string of bad checks to neighborhood merchants. The theater, featuring drag contests where men dressed as women paraded on stage winning a $15 check (that also bounced), was to be the first of a string of such movie houses in the nation.

According to the police, the theater was actually owned by an eastern syndicate, in fact the hoodlum boss came to San Francisco recently to see what could be done to save the investment.

But the heat was on. After mounting neighborhood pressure, a series of blistering editorials in the Independent and even a picket line by youngsters, the syndicate decided they had enough.

One of the owners, Bart Smith, was arrested last week when he falsely charged a group of heckling youngsters of robbing his theater. He was to appear in court but skipped bail and fled.

This should alert hoodlums that an aroused community will not tolerate vultures of this type.[5]

For all practical purposes, then, when the new population that was to become the Hippies began to arrive in 1965, what they came to was essentially "a liberal, sometimes radical, successfully integrated, bohemian, working class, deviant, residential area."

## THE TWO POPULATIONS

By 1965 it was apparent to the old residents of the Haight-Ashbury that the population composition of the District was again changing. These changes were noticeable particularly in the Panhandle and in the area of Golden Gate Park adjacent to Haight Street, as well as on Haight Street itself. The first perceptible change was the fact that there were more than the ordinary number of white youths in the area.[6] The fact was commented on by the District leaders in the Neighborhood Council with pleasure. They said, essentially, that it was "nice to see young faces in the area" and they stated explicitly to one another that it would be good if such young people decided to stay in the District; it would "revitalize the neighborhood, bring a sense of life to it."

The second change in the District, in terms of the development of what was to be eventually called the "New Community," was the opening of an explicitly bohemian coffee house, with decor and trappings to proclaim it as such. (The "New Community" was first used as a term to designate the contrast with the "Old Community" which was composed of everyone who used to live in the District. This designation was employed until about 1966.)

The owner of the coffee house requested membership and

was welcomed into the Haight-Ashbury Neighborhood Merchants Association within a few months after the coffee house opened.

The influx of the new population of white youths in their late teens and early 20's continued gradually. In a sense, this influx occurred both perceptibly and imperceptibly for the "Old Community." The change was perceptible insofar as the "Old Community" was in general aware that "there were more young people in the neighborhood"; it was also imperceptible in that apparently the "Old Community" never thought about the extent of the new population, or about how the character of the new population was itself changing.

Whether or not it was perceived by the "Old Community," this initial change in the new population had a very visible aspect —a change in costume. At first, the dress of the new population was in no way notable. It included a sprinkling of persons in bright "psychedelic" colored clothing: bell-bottom pants, paisley shirts and dresses. About the time that the color of their dress began to make the extent of the population visible to the "Old Community," a number of "New Community" shops were opened on Haight Street.

For the most part, these were dry goods stores catering to the tastes of the "New Community." However, when the entrepreneurs of the new shops applied to the Haight-Ashbury Neighborhood Merchants' Association for membership, they were turned down, the established merchants claiming that the new entrepreneurs were, in effect, "irresponsible."

Regardless of whether there was any perceived cleavage between the "Old Community" and the "New Community" before this, the incident served to divide the population of the District into these two mutually self-identified communities. Each put forth a claim for the geographical area. The Old Community essentially made its argument on the grounds that they were there first, that they owned property, paid taxes, supported and were concerned about the problems of the schools and traffic, and that generally they were involved in all the other matters of conventional civic concern. The claim of the New Community was that they were there *now*.

This general argument of the new residents is illustrated by the following excerpts from field observations in the summer of 1966.

> I have been sharing a table and a conversation with four Hippies in one of the coffee houses. The general topic has been the Hippies' feeling that the old residents are not willing to acknowledge the former's rights in the District. I mention that perhaps the feeling on the part of the old residents is that the new residents refuse to assist the old residents in managing the problems of the neighborhood, such as the school situation, which has been an ongoing source of trouble in the neighborhood for years.
>
> One of the Hippies states, "That's their problem" and goes on to say that the new residents "have a right to be left alone because we're here."

The New Community entrepreneurs who had been denied membership to the Merchants' Association responded by forming their own association, The Hip Independent Proprietors. This, combined with the sense of animosity on the part of the Old Community, was apparently sufficient to provide a core around which a collectivity of people could identify themselves as an independent community. By the latter part of 1966 the terms "Old Community" and "New Community" were rarely heard; they were replaced by the terms: "The Straights" and "The Hippies." [7]

## THE HIPPIE COMMUNITY

In the latter part of 1965 and the early part of 1966 a number of changes began to take place in the new residents who were to become the Hippie community. The bright, psychedelic clothing became a widespread phenomenon, virtually a uniform. It then merged into the era of the "costume." The "costume" (or as it was occasionally called, "high costume") was just that: any outfit or part of an outfit from a different temporal era or a different geographical place: flowing eastern robes, uniforms that looked like those worn by Civil War officers, American Indian feathers, Victorian morning dresses, or 1930 evening gowns. At the same time the ranks of the Haight-Ashbury residents began to include the Hell's Angels, who fit into the area easily on the basis of appearance (since they too routinely wore a unique "costume" of their own). The Hell's Angels were also compatible on the basis of their acceptance and use of drugs and their beliefs about the members of the conventional society.

Also at this time, the number of Hippie shops along Haight Street increased substantially. By the end of 1966 there were about thirty establishments in the District that were generally acknowledged as "belonging" to the Hippie community. There were mainly psychedelic notions stores selling buttons, posters, jewelry, and various "trip toys"; sandal makers' shops; clothing stores; art supply stores; and coffee houses. About the same time, a number of take-out food stalls opened in the street, apparently catering to a highly transient population of both Hippies and tourists.

Through late 1965 and into 1966, the relationship between the Hippie community and the Straight community in the District had much the appearance of a standoff. For the most part, the old leaders of the Straight community, (still actively maintaining the Neighborhood Council) perceived themselves as in an ideological bind. They felt that they did not understand the Hippies and they also knew that they did not like what they saw of Hippie life in its public settings. They felt, as well, that they were losing their neighborhood. But their own self-conscious ideology, their own self-defined and valued "liberality," served to prohibit them from taking decisive offensive action against the Hippies. As "liberals," they saw themselves obligated to tolerate the way of life others preferred, and the obligation remained even if they did not understand nor approve of this life. As believers themselves in the ideology of community (albeit, the variety generated within the framework of left politics), they could see no reason to enforce their claim on the locale by actively excluding the

Hippies. They acknowledged that they owned property, paid taxes, and had a general civic concern and that the Hippies did not. But they also saw that this did not necessarily give them an explicit mandate to those areas they did not specifically "own": the streets, the parks, the individual shops along Haight Street.

A few attempts were made on the part of the Neighborhood Council and one of the churches to bring the two communities together, with the hope of eventually reaching some sort of satisfactory relationship between them. The Neighborhood Council occasionally invited the members of the Hip Merchants (and through them, their patrons) to the Council meetings, but few came. One of the churches invited members of the Neighborhood Council and the Hip Merchants to a specially formed "conciliation committee" meeting. Members of both groups showed up in about equal numbers, but the meeting ended (after more than two hours) with a sense of futility on both sides. The following field excerpts from that meeting provide an example of the kind of "talking past" one another that characterized the entire meeting:

> The participants from both sides are in general "airing complaints and grudges" they have concerning the other side. Tom, a middle-aged Black Straight (who has lived in the district for at least seven or eight years), says angrily, "I don't like it when you abuse my wife. That's what I don't like. If you wouldn't abuse our women, we wouldn't be so angry with you." Ken, a Hip merchant, says to Tom: "What do you mean?" Tom answers, "You sit in the doorways [of the stores on Haight Street] and make remarks—make her walk around you." Ken answers, "I thought you said we abused her, and you did." It is never resolved, at least at this table, whether the Straights and the Hippies are mutually to consider "abuse" as constituting "making remarks and crowding doorways." The issue is dropped.
>
> Somewhat later, Bill, a middle-aged white resident of the neighborhood for about four years, says with a tone of astonishment (which I later come to realize is his style of presenting his annoyance): "Do you know what happened in the flat right across the street from me? That I can see from my window? There were two Hippies, making love. On the porch. Outside. You could see

it from my window." One of the Hip merchants responds,
"What's wrong with making love?" Bill repeats, with studious
precision, "Outside?" The Hip merchant responds in turn, "So
what?" It continues like this for almost twenty minutes, and then,
like the problem of what constitutes "abuse," the problem of
whether making love in public is "improper" also dies out.

Caught in the implications of their own ideological com-
mitments, the Straights eventually gave up. They would frequently
complain to one another about how despicable the way of life of
the Hippies was in general. And they would complain about how
the Hippies made shopping on Haight Street difficult, if not im-
possible—about how the Hippies were "ruining" the District. In
public encounters with the Hippies, in the parks, on the street,
and especially in the doorways to the Straight shops on Haight
Street, they would treat the Hippies as non-persons. In effect, the
only decisive action ever undertaken with respect to the presence
of the Hippies in the area was to put large wrought-iron gates
on the doorways of the Straight resident flats that faced on Haight
Street and other streets heavily used by Hippies.

At the same time, through the Neighborhood Council, any
offensive action the city took toward the Hippies was heatedly
protested by the leaders of the Straight community (as when the
Health Department made an unprecedented check on the residents
of the neighborhood, ostensibly to provide legal grounds for
evicting the Hippies). Having, albeit passively, acknowledged the
right of the Hippie community to exist in the District, they apparently now felt obligated to defend its civil rights as well.

By the middle of 1966 there was no longer any concerted
opposition to the Hippie community, at least within the immediate
area. Opposition on the part of individual Straight residents apparently continued, but not as a part of any collective enterprise.
Sporadic attempts at "containing the situation" came from "downtown": a sudden Public Health inspection; the increase in the
number of policemen on foot in the neighborhood; the increase
in the number of police patrol cars; and the increase of policemen

in patrol cars in the Haight-Ashbury from two per car to three.

One might almost say that the Hippies had conquered the area. Certainly they now recognized it as "their" territory; and their recognition was eventually supplemented by the recognition of the mass media. For the media, the Haight-Ashbury District and the Hippie movement were for the most part one and the same. However, some place along the way the name of the District was changed. For the Straight residents it remained "The Haight-Ashbury." For the media, it became "The Hashbury." For the Hippies, it eventually came to be called simply "The Haight."

In the present chapter, I have attempted to specify some of the courses of social action which took place in the Haight-Ashbury District prior to and concurrent with the appearance of the Hippies. In the ongoing stream of phenomenal time, the signs which mark historical eras and historical places (as socially perceived events) are neither noted in advance of their coming (like the signs heralding freeway exits) nor are they necessarily definitive and explicit in the information they proclaim (like the association of flags with the country they signify). For the observer, history is constantly changing; while for those observed, the world is perceived either as the same as it has always been, or different from "before." Thus, as a general methodological problem, it does not seem sufficient to assume that everything that might be relevant to the interpretation of the data about an historical group begins at the point in time when the researcher begins his observations. For the social actors, there is some meaningful referent to "before." I have tried in the present chapter to describe salient features of that "before" as it bears specifically on the existence of the Hippie community as an empirical phenomenon.

The existence of the Hippie community as an observable social fact on the American scene was a matter acknowledged by both members and non-members alike. Many courses of action, like tributary streams of behavior, fed into the establishment of the community as a social fact. As I have suggested in the foregoing sections, some of the salient events included the passive acceptance of the Hippies by the Straights in the District; the apparent recognition of the Hippies on the part of the conventional society as a whole; and the Hippies own self-recognition of themselves as a community.

The courses of social action which preceded the community of Hippies might be expressed as the process of persons homesteading an area. Such a demographic population flow began in the Haight-Ashbury District of San Francisco in 1965. It began with the arrival of (what was then considered) undefinable non-conventional youths.

By 1966 those who had recently begun to reside in the District became identified as the "New Community." The New Community was perceivably differentiated from the residents of the Old Community in the District in a variety of ways. The members of the Old Community were generally in their forties; the members of the New Community were in their twenties. The racial composition of the Old Community was more than half Negro; the members of the New Community were almost exclusively white. The members of the Old Community were regular workers; the members of the New Community worked only occasionally, if at all. Ecologically, in terms of the service and facilities available in the District, there were some (such as the parks, the buses, grocery stores, as well as dwelling units) that were used by members of both communities. There were other facilities (such as the public library, the notary publics, the banks, and churches) that were utilized almost solely by the members of the Old Community. Ultimately, there were new facilities that were oriented nearly exclusively to members of the New Community.

As those persons engaged in the process of "homesteading" eventually became recognized as a discrete collectivity in their own right, the individual members of the collectivity took on a more or less general identity. Thus, at some point in time (c. 1966), the District quite clearly had been staked out as an area "belonging" to some identifiable group—a group which had a clearly different population make-up from the natives who also still lived there. And equally clearly, the new group had different interests and a different style of life from the natives. Eventually, the group was identified by the designation "Hippie," a term that could refer alternatively to the members of the group (as when a member of the Old Community would indicate a person by saying, "Oh, he's one of those 'Hippies' ") or any part of the life (as when shops were designated as "Hippie places").

By the time the group came to be identified as the Hippie community, there was concurrently present an identifiable ideology which was regularly associated with the collectivity, and which was accepted by persons who claimed membership in that community. Thus, concurrent with the Hippie community as a social fact was the Hippie ideology as a social fact.

## NOTES

1. Nelson Goodman, *The Structure of Appearance* (Indianapolis, Ind.: The Bobbs-Merrill Co., 1966), pp. 9–13.

2. In 1960, the racial composition of the six census tracts which approximate the district boundaries included 21 percent Black and 8 percent other non-white. (U.S. Census of Population and Housing: 19 Final Report PHC(1)–137, Bureau of the Census, Washington, D.C.) These latter were primarily Chinese, although there have also been a substantial number of Filipinos living in the District in the earlier part of the decade.

3. According to informants familiar with North Beach during the 1950's, the Haight-Ashbury was in effect one of three districts in the city that migrants from the earlier bohemias selected in substantial numbers in the early part of the 1960's.

4. The theater was reopened in 1967 as a site for Hippie "happenings." At that time the name of the theater was changed from "The Haight" to "The Straight," which may have been chosen as a rhyming modification of the previous name, as a dig at the Straight residents, or as an indirect reference to its previous existence as a "gay" theater.

5. *Haight-Ashbury Independent,* August 20, 1964.

6. In 1960, in the six census tracts of the District, white youths be-

tween the ages of fifteen and twenty-four numbered 3,427. (U.S. Census, *op. cit.*, pp. 126–127). Fred Davis' estimate of the Hippie population in the District in 1967 was 7,500. "Why All of Us May Be Hippies Someday," *trans*action, Vol. 5 (December, 1967), p. 10.

7. Cf. Leonard Wolf, *Voices of the Love Generation* (Boston: Little, Brown & Co., 1968).

# 4

# The Hippie Community
# as a System of Beliefs

A working knowledge of the Hippie ideology is requisite for those who claim bona-fide membership in the Hippie community of the Haight—for those who identify themselves and who are acknowledged as Hippies. What do these credentials require? First of all, if paying allegiance to a group (by claiming bona-fide membership) is to be more than a ritual to the individual person, he must have some general (even though only partial) understanding of what membership means. Furthermore, if he cares at all to be taken as a member by others, he must know what members are expected to believe. This knowledge is requisite if he is to make statements about his beliefs that will seem convincing to the uninformed, and correct to the informed.

In order to answer questions of "what members believe," the Hippies of the Haight may respond by asserting such things as,
Hippies believe:

..... that man should be free
..... that man's psyche can set him free
..... that drugs can set man's psyche free
..... that no individual free man could act in a way to jeopardize his freedom

..... that beauty and freedom are one and the same
..... that the realization of all of the above is a spiritual matter
..... that all those people who realize the above form a spiritual
        community
..... that that spiritual community can be nothing other than
        ideal
..... that all the above is the truth
..... and that those who believe otherwise are mistaken

However, when a member is called on to inform the uninformed what membership "means," he may choose to indicate
various things that "members do." He may indicate "what members do" in two ways. First, he can proclaim one of a number of
moral maxims embedded within the ideology as a matter of
common social knowledge. For a Hippie of the Haight, "what a
good Hippie does" is to follow such moral maxims as "Do your
own thing," "Don't bum-trip anyone," "Don't hassle," "Share."
However, "what a good Hippie does" is a matter of folk wisdom,
to be understood as "more or less the case." In this sense, the
uninformed must understand (as matters unspoken) that

(1) *obviously,* not all Hippies are Good Hippies; and (2)
that *anyone* knows just what things will be sanctioned by other
members; that (3) *clearly,* there is difference between "a favor"
which can be requested and "a bummer" which is not to be imposed.

A second way of indicating "what Hippies do," is by generally describing the kind of practices in which Hippies engage. Or,
a description can be given by actually showing the uninformed
the life as a guided guest. Thus, the uninformed may be presented
directly with what membership means by being presented (as a
description or a fact) with everyday Hippie practices. However,
what the uninformed may make of those activities is not always
perfectly clear; and he may ask his host for an interpretation. In
providing the guest with an *interpretation* of the activities of the
group—in explaining the meaning of "what Hippies are doing"—
members are required to employ some part of the ideology as a

framework of interpretation. Such a framework serves to "locate" the symbolic meaning of the particular practices in question. Thus, for the uninformed to "fully understand" (to a member's satisfaction) the practices he is told about, witnesses, or joins in, he must see their symbolic side as well. He must see how those practices are representative instances of a cultured way of life—in the sense that those practices are "refined" or made clearer by the ideological significance attributed to them.

Thus, it will be assumed that any member's assertion about "what members believe" is always a summary statement of elements in a more embracing or comprehensive scheme of things. When a member acts as "philosopher," his beliefs are not matters of justifying decisions for action, but matters of contemplation. They are not now to be evoked as the grounds for action, but reflected upon. For the observing-member, it is not only segments of actual action which may be considered in terms of their general patterning and organization; but also beliefs about action which may be so considered. Thus, like a description of the "way of life," a description of the "world view" constitutes a systemization of segments of immediately relevant matters.[1] The purpose of the present chapter is to describe the salient features of the "comprehensive scheme of things" as "the Hippie Ideology."

In the same sense, beliefs are practical premises for the members. Their beliefs provide justifiable grounds to choose between alternative courses of action in coming to terms with the circumstances of their life. Such "practical beliefs" do not require that they be seen as either integrated or coherent systems, since at any given moment of decision, not all those beliefs will be relevant to the possibilities of action available for any given member.

The various segments of the ideology are present and available for the participating-members of the community. However, these particular beliefs are not necessarily seen as a systematically organized "philosophy of life." Rather, they are "seen" as beliefs relevant to the practical circumstances of action, evoked as the members perceive the warrant for them.

In removing beliefs from the context of ongoing action, I have transformed them from particular declarations of "what members proclaim they believe" into a general "philosophical system of beliefs." This construction is necessary since one does not encounter the entire "way of life" at any given moment in a community as might be presented by an ethnographer. Neither does one encounter the entire "philosophy of life" explained by any given member as it is constructed and ultimately presented by a philosopher. Both the "way of life" and the "philosophy of life" are *reflective* composites.[2] They are constructed by taking the particular segments of action and the particular assertions of belief and organizing them into a general description.[3]

What is relevant to the description as an adequate formulation of the actual assertions of beliefs of a group that members make, is that the final summary description of the assertion be comprehensible to members. In effect, the criterion for an adequate description of the way of life is that members can recognize it and say, "Yes, that is the way we believe around here." [4]

Within the context of the present study, the ideology of the Hippies—the conscious beliefs of the members—is taken as critical for a sociological analysis of the Hippie community. I have accepted the following assumption in formulating the overview of this ideology: The ideological assertions Hippies make in the ongoing course of their everyday life are taken to be the "actual beliefs" members hold. Such assertions include what they say about what they believe to each other and to anyone they come into contact with during their ongoing round of everyday activity.[5] In addition to such assertions contained in my records of field observations, I have included ideological assertions made by members during the course of a series of unstructured interviews from 1967. These interviews were edited and published by Leonard Wolf in *Voices of the Love Generation*.[6] Thus the data from which the description of the Hippie ideology has been constructed include what members say to one another (as observed during their ongoing daily round) and what members assert to outsiders (as recorded in the Wolf interviews). My purpose for including these published examples is to provide additional evidence for the adequacy of the ideological description. That is to say, if we take the situation of an-interview-for-a-book-to-be-published-about-Hippies as one where members are most apt to see themselves as being "on," [7] we would assume the interviewed would give the most idealized version they can provide of the actual matters discussed. Such an idealized version in this context would be a version which they would assume other competent members sanction as constituting "what a competent Hippie would say." What they tell outsiders about their life should thus be an excellent indicator of what they assume other competent members would also say.

## FEATURES OF THE HIPPIE IDEOLOGY

### A. *The Vision*

For the Hippies of the Haight, the world begins and ends with, literally, a vision.[8] One becomes aware of the world simultaneously with becoming aware of one's own psyche.

One's psyche in this sense is constituted of the consciousness of possibilities, the ability to formulate images of things not given in the present moment of sensory awareness.[9]

> Paul, in explaining what it is like to "really see" the world says, "You're looking at a glass of water and seeing it not just as a glass of water but as a glass of water *and* something to drink *and* crystal clarity *and* the seas *and* the rain *and* the rainbow."
>
> He goes on to say that once you have realized that all of those possibilities are always there, then you've "really" seen a glass of water for the first time.
>
> "I did it in the beginning (taken acid for mind-expansion) to see how far I could stretch my head. To see how far I could take an idea, and things like that. . . . There's a whole period when

you're just starting to take acid when you're getting used to it. Every time you watch some different way of reacting to things. Every once in a while you watch yourself going through very egotistical patterns of behavior. And you kind of stand back and realize you've done this an awful lot, and you see it from an entirely different perspective. I never really got into using it that way." [10]

In a very Cartesian sense, the consciousness of alternative possibilities to the present moment of sensory awareness makes these alternatives as "real" as the present moment. The vision thus consists of the realization of the simultaneity of mind and matter (thought and sensory experience) as the reality of the here and now.

A small group of Hippies are sitting in the park, talking in general about the "Straights," and the "Straights' lack of understanding about the world." At one point, one of the group says, of the Straights, "They think that if you imagine something that you can't touch it's a hallucination. . . . They'll never understand that ideas are real too."

"After my first acid trip, I was overwhelmed with the importance of imagination. I suddenly saw how key imagination was to sanity. That in some ways you could define a problem as limited alternatives, all of which are unacceptable. But in reality, there are infinite alternatives. . . . Everything is real. Human beings can invent unreal things, they can think of unreal things. It's all real. It's all right here." [11]

The "can" and the "could," the "is" and the "is not" are all elements of one's psychic consciousness. This is, in effect, the vision.

The sense of the vision—its meaning—is resolved into an unquestioned acceptance of "total reality" as a matter of the conjunction of the physical world and the psychic world. The physical world is, in Wittgenstein's terms, "all that is the case" and what is the case—an empirical fact—is the existence of sensate states of affairs.[12] The psychic world is an attitude, a perspective, a particular choice of how to order and arrange the elements of the physical world. Thus, any particular "picture" one has of the physical world is dependent upon where one chooses to stand to look at what there is to see; how one chooses to arrange such "states of affairs."

Bart says to me, "I want to be in control of my ideas instead of my ideas being in control of me. I am here (he puts out one hand) and my ideas are here (he puts out his other hand, a little away from the first one and a little in front of it). If you look from here, it looks like this hand (the first one) is causing this hand (the second one)." (The "here" is a perspective in which both hands appear to be part of the same continuous plane.)

"But if you look from here, they are not the same at all." (This "here" is a perspective in which the hands appear to be located on separate planes and on points not coordinated between those planes.)

"LSD puts you in touch with your surroundings. You take LSD and your surroundings are there. Feelings about your surroundings are there. The onion is peeled and peeled and peeled and in the center we have something that is really an incredible thing. It's where we're able to see from more accurately, and more honestly, and without a great deal of incredible amounts of effort . . . (the use of these drugs) automatically puts people in a different frame of reference. It points out a lot of inequities in the system. Just by their existence; by the fact that they are suppressed. . . ." [13]

Man is thus seen to be "free" in the sense that he can transcend the immediate moment of sensate awareness by imagining alternative arrangements. The "necessity" of the world as it has always been apprehended dissolves into an open vista of possibilities. What is equally important is that man is free to act upon these imagined alternatives. By his actions, man can bring about as sensate states of affairs any psychic possibility he can imagine.

Howard and some others have talked about what it is like to be on acid. At one point Howard turns to me and says, "I tried to play chess on acid one time. You can't. You see the board and there are a million possibilities (to make a move) and all of them are beautiful. I mean, you can move a piece, but you realize you could move any piece and play any number of games you want to." I ask him what he means by this and he goes on to explain that if you really wanted to you could play a conventional game of chess. But there is no necessity to it; you could also play a countless number of games which would be variations on the game of chess as it is customarily played.

"You move around a lot. We're just out to turn everyone on. You're always up against the Man. You want to do beautiful things that you know are beautiful. You want to have a permit to have a fire in an open lot, so you can have a barbecue. You look at the ground, you look at the air where the fire would be. You know where the fire hoses are, you know there's no problem. Everyone knows it. But in comes the fire inspector, regulation twenty, you've got to have two exits. You don't have that. No fire . . . because of a foolish, obscene, ridiculous regulation that has nothing to do with the facts of the matter. You run into this all the time. You smoke marijuana, you know that marijuana is a good healthy thing for a human being to do. While you're doing this good healthy thing, you want to share it with your friend. (But) you've got this eye, this ominous presence, lurking around. It wants to put you in jail for doing what you know is a good thing to do. . . . That's my day. Now somebody is going to say, 'Well, why don't you just obey the law?' Well, I don't know why it's there. What I do know is the Vietnamese are dying for what they believe in and all the technology and might and truth in the world isn't going to stop them." [14]

The vision and its concomitant realization of man's freedom is an individual event which occurs for individual men. No one can "give" the vision to another. At most, one can attempt to bring about the conditions which encourage the possibility that another will have the vision too.[15]

Michael and some others have been engaged in talking about the drug experience. It is one of the most constant topics of conversation. This evening the focus of the conversation has been how the drug experience results in the users "understanding" about what the world is "really like."

I ask Michael if somebody could come to the same understanding about the world without drugs, and he answers yes, cit-ing some Yogis and other mystics who, he says, "understand the world in the same way after meditating." But then he goes on to add. "You know, it's a very personal thing. You have to see it yourself. . . . Nobody can tell anybody else about it."

When I ask why not, he becomes a little impatient with me and says, "If you don't see it for yourself, you can never understand what somebody else is rapping (talking) about."

"Like in music, like I always play flute on the street and stuff, and try to turn the Straight people on. . . . 'Cause I know I'm doin' better'n them, and I would like to bring what I know is better—not better, but a different world. . . ." [16]

## B. *The Given Situation*

The circumstances of man's life are thus presented in the simultaneous presence of the physical world and the consciousness of the possibilities that exist within that world. Like the immediate moment of the sensory awareness of the physical world, the consciousness of the possible arrangements of that world are not a matter of some speculative future, but a matter of the present here and now.[17]

Insofar as the first cause and final basis of the given situation is one's psychic awareness, consciousness constitutes the crux of existence.

Eric says, quite suddenly, "My mind is the most beautiful thing in the whole world because that's where the whole world is."

The rest of the group respond by laughing, but it seems that they are laughing more at the sudden solemnity and awe of Eric's proclamation than at what he has said specifically.

A few days later, someone who had been in the group that night, in talking about Eric, says, "Eric really knows where it is at."

"If you don't want the world you're pushed into, you have to find another world. You can't sit back and say it's all going to work out. No exterior movement can function unless it's composed of people whose interior is fit. . . . The first place that it has to happen is inside. You learn where you are. You learn if you want to make it here or in the trees. You learn if you want to make it with men or with women or play with yourself. You learn not because this is the way it's supposed to be, but truthfully, in yourself it's what you want." [18]

Yet, consciousness does not exist without form and substance. The form of consciousness is embodied in action and the content of consciousness is embodied in sensate and psychic experience.

> Bob starts to tell the three of us about a rather serious accident he had some time ago, while he was on acid. He goes on and says, "On acid I had to learn to acknowledge vanity. I mean, I was all hung up on being vain . . . wanted to cleanse myself of it. That's when I fell out of the window. I saw (then) that you couldn't not be vain. That's you and if that isn't part of the world, then there's no world."
> Somewhat later he says, "I look at my feet. Beautiful. I love my feet. That's where I end. It's good to know where you end."

> "I'm very conscious of my social entity. The animal I am. I have needs: food, clothing, and shelter. But I also have a desire to spread out my energies, to pour them into beautiful things, into beautiful people. Into raising their levels, and mine, because we all raise them together.
> "I frankly believe in the Haight. . . . I live love, I live peace, I live beauty." [19]

It is understood that a man will act only in ways which will not jeopardize his freedom, given his psychic awareness of his life circumstances. And by definition, such action cannot result in anything but aesthetic and spiritual beauty.

> Nora has been telling me about the changes which have taken place in her life in the past few years, particularly as they are related to the use of acid and peyote. At one point she says, "I saw so clearly that there's no point in trying to control your life."
> She goes on to expand on this, explaining that if you just let yourself do what you feel intuitively is right, it will be right. But if you try to plan ahead and think it all out before you act—if you go against your intuition—you will probably make a mistake.

> Q: "You accept the idea that you have a right to be physically beautiful?"

Ron: "Sure, (you) should be. Because everybody is. The more you're yourself, the more you really fill up and relax, listen, give. The more you're yourself, the more beautiful you are. And everybody is the most interesting person in the world. Every person is." [20]

## C. *The Psychic Community*

Each individual's realization of the "true" circumstances of man's life can only result in action which is both free and beautiful. In this way, a spiritual community of visionaries is possible on the basis of each individual making the *same* discovery.

David suggests that we go to the beach in Marin. I suggest that we might go to the one here in the city, since it is much closer. David says no, because the particular beach he wants to go to is the one which is, in effect, Hippie territory and he says that "it can't help but be a good day with *them*." The implication that his remarks carry is that Hippies, by definition, are compatible and harmonious. This is a statement that I have heard from a variety of people on a variety of occasions. Sometimes it is put as "our people."

"I feel that they're (the Haight-Ashbury) my people. Like when we were traveling . . . to see someone who was obviously a Hippie was a marvelous thing, because it was instant communication, instant love, and helping . . . but when you're down on Montgomery Street walking and you see all the really poor people who are on their half-hour lunch break and are uptight, unhappy, in debt—the middle-class Montgomery Street employees . . . that their suits all look alike. And to see a Hippie down there, as soon as you see one, there's this instant big smile and happy vibration, and wonderful communication." [21]

The love of one's individual self can no longer be separated from the love of other selves, insofar as there are no longer any perceivable differences between self and other. Both self and other share the same consciousness and the same situation.

Thus, by definition, the psychic community must be a utopia. Even though each individual member constructs his personal world as he so desires, his actions will never jeopardize the freedom of either himself or others, nor be anything but beautiful for others. The system always works since the community is constituted in the first place by individual men with the same vision and hence the same circumstances. It is a spiritual community of men—a community that is not encountered as a fact external to each individual man, but rather encountered as a fact internal to each member. It is a community constituted by individual psyches joined into one.

The tribe exemplifies the spiritual community, for in the tribe, all members know all there is to be known.[22]

> Five of us have been sitting around, listening to the radio and occasionally talking. I mention at one point Freuchen's *Book of the Eskimos,* saying that I find the way of life of the Eskimos very fascinating. Helen asks me what that way of life is like and I recount some ethnographic descriptions in it. When I am done, Stan says "That's the way it should be. Everybody should know the same thing and then they would live in peace."
>
> I don't quite understand the relevance of Stan's remark at that point. When I bring it up again two or three days later, Stan says I said the Eskimos were a tribe, and that's the way people should live, although I did not in fact say anything about the Eskimos being a tribe, but only having organized their life in a particular kind of way.

> "Tribal identity comes because you want to trust each other. It's one of the things I realized at one of the (Be-Ins) in (Golden Gate Park). There were a great number of people there that I could trust with my life. Because they were people that belonged to me and I belonged to them. It's an instinctual, non-intellectual response. Now the tribal thing is very hard to define, because it's a very strange culture we're in. A lot of this stuff is camp. Like I don't think wearing a headband, and playing Indians, or any of these things means anything at all. Like it's a game. There's a lot of deadweight to it, too. There's kids that are just playing for a while. They've run away from home, and they're going to go back home. I just hope that they carry with them what trust means, and what mutual care means. That's what the tribe is: people that are taking care of each other for real. Who care about each other.

Who are mutually responsible for each other. Lovingly. Willingly. Who feel that sense of the tribe. You feel it when you know it. It doesn't come from the outside really." [23]

Reality is thus constructed by "cutting" the world in a horizontal plane, rather than a vertical one. The community of man is not a collectivity where the individual members share in common a psychic life *and* a physical world. Such a collectivity is not considered a "spiritual" community by members; for they perceive themselves separated by virtue of the particular conjunction of the psychic-and-physical segment that is "theirs." [24] Rather, the "spiritual community of man" is a collectivity where the individual members all share in common the same psychic life vis-à-vis the same physical world.[25]

## D. *The Universe*

The apprehension of the true community of man as a spiritual community is made when the vision (of alternative possibilities) is contrasted with the present conditions of mankind. The universe is thus a meta-realization, in which the original vision is seen from the perspective of the ultimate insight.

> It
> the thing for which I have no name
> completes the perfect circle perfectly
> just beyond the barricades of flesh
> called ego, encompassing the senses
> and the intellect in fierce imagination
> and mirage
>
> and I am paradoxed
> by matter itself
> dromedary dream of the universe.[26]

The ultimate insight—the insight of "the full realization of the insight of the first vision"—resolves all questions. There is nothing more to be shown, although from this realization there is much to be concluded.

Bart has been playing a kind of hide-and-go-seek with me (what Linda refers to, the next night, as "not really putting you on," even though it has the appearance of that). He "makes a point" by bringing two events together and, once I have acknowledged them, dropping one of the original events and taking up a third, showing me that it is all really very different. I finally ask him. "What are you talking about?" He responds, "What do you mean, what am I talking about?" as though I should "surely" be able to see, as though it were all obvious.

I try to explain that it will take me a while to figure out what he is talking about—that I know the world through the analysis of a series of discrete events. Bart responds that I am "not with it." He goes on to say that to "really understand" I would just "immediately understand"; I would just see it instead of having to break it into parts before I could put it together to see "what it is." I ask how I can know that what I see right now (or at any given moment) will be the same as what he sees. But this is an irrelevant remark on my part; Bart treats it as a nonsense-noise, simply ignoring it and rapping on about something else.

On other occasions, when I have asked the same question, I have received the reply: "You just know, you're on the same wave length, getting the same vibrations and you know it."

"The common reaction of people who get high the first time is 'Wow! Is that real? Is that what's really happening? Wow! Did you see it? It's real!' Not a specimen world anymore. It's not a consumer-conveyor, consumer-conveyor-sit-in-a-slot-boom-boom-boom-boom-boom-boom-boom-boom-boom-boom-FEED-boom-boom-boom-boom-SHIT-boom-boom-boom-SLEEP-boom-boom. It's not like that. It's like sentences don't have so many periods, it's like getting more dashes and colons and commas and involutions." [27]

When the possibilities of how mankind's life is to be lived (as they are presented in the vision) are compared with any particular way of life (as it is presented in the given situation), some ways of life can be seen to be harmonious and others inharmonious.

The true way of life is the way of life in which man and

nature live in harmony; the false way of life is when man and nature live in conflict.

"There's a very strong identification in the Haight-Ashbury (with the American Indians) as we play out our Karmic roles and go through our evolution in our previous incarnations . . . And the American Indian is the Indian-Human Being, brave warrior, who had a good relationship with the land which we find missing today and which is a good part of the rebellion that was mentioned before . . ." [28]

The ultimate insight is the ultimate insight because it is the final boundary of reason. Any insight concerning the insight concerning the insight of the vision resolves the universe into absurdity.

I have sent a friend in the community an earlier paper I had written, on the analysis of the Hippie beliefs about form and ritual. In the letter I received from him in response, he comments on his impression of the activities of the Hippies in the District and some of his own recent experiences, ending by writing: "Words seem almost impotent against such a profound sensual experience (such as that of acid). Maybe it's a paradox to discuss the life of form since the act mitigates all discussion."

"Okay, so it's not new. So one day the universe might disappear into the wink of God's eye. And start all over again with some explosion. It doesn't concern me. The Communists say the root of everything is dialectical materialism, uh-huh. The Jehovah Witnesses say the root of everything is destruction by fire, uh-huh. Everybody has their own frame. It's a big goddam planet. It includes every frame you can think of. Every tangent. Every opposite. Every travesty. Every permutation. Every practical joke. Every shade. Everything you want to talk about. That's not to say you can't see things clearly. I think you can." [29]

In effect, the three-valued logic can be carried out only to two places in the search for final truth, for final truth, to be both final and true, must be stable. One can know (have the vision), one can know that one knows (have the insight of vision), but to know that you know that you know tumbles into an infinite regress for which there is no stop-rule.[30]

## THE MORAL MAXIMS

In the preceding pages, I have tried to survey the salient features of the Hippie ideology. The description of that ideology has been presented as the "background matters" against which any singular assertion concerning "what members believe" is to be generally understood.

The substance of the Hippie ideology contains a variety of moral maxims as it is discussed on a day-to-day basis. However, the sensible character of these maxims is apprehended only when they are understood in terms of the general belief system of which they are a part.[31] The precept "Do your own thing," for example, is a meaningful principle of moral conduct only insofar as it is understood that in "doing one's own thing" one is freely implementing the possibilities of action that are open to him and that any collectivity of men sharing the given situation will comprehend it in the same way. Hence, there is no way in which the individual action of one individual man doing his own thing can conflict with the action taken by the collectivity of other men doing their own thing.

Such ideological maxims are in effect summary statements of the general ideology: the knowledge of the precept implying, as a background, the knowledge of the system of beliefs of which it is a part. As summary statements, the maxims provide members with the most succinct formulations of the belief system they acknowledge. They also contain the most explicit propositions about action-to-be-taken-in-accordance-with-one's-beliefs. Yet in no sense are these maxims themselves direct ideological "commands" for members to act. Understanding the social actions that the precepts justify requires a concomitant understanding of the belief system of which they are a part. In the same way, the translation of these maxims into actual ongoing courses of action for members requires interpreting the general belief system as a means of seeing the "correctness" of any particular decision.[32]

As I have suggested in Chapter I, members "see" the correctness of any practical instance of action by interpreting between their ideological beliefs and the actual activities of themselves and others. If one is to employ "Do your own thing" as a principle of conduct, the knowledge that one has employed it correctly rests upon knowing what things are to count as "things" [33] Novitiate members may be provided with a list of maxims such as "Do your own thing" to teach them what their world is all about. But they are rarely, if ever, provided with the corresponding list of "things that are sanctioned 'things'" so that all they need do is match what they are doing with what is on the list to know the correctness of their activity.[34]

Thus, if members of the Hippie community are to conduct their everyday affairs in a way that will be both sensible and sanctioned by other members, they must do so despite the fact that the ideology provides them with no clearly posited rule to follow. Furthermore, if asked what the rules of the Hippie community are, members will insist that there are none.[35] Or, they will respond with statements such as "A Hippie is someone who just does his own thing." As a moral maxim, such an assertion has the sound of a rule; of a practical guide to actual conduct. But it is imprecise and ambiguous. Even to the casual observer, it is quite obvious that not "everything" will stand in the community as a sanctioned "Hippie thing." During the course of their practical affairs, the Hippies of the Haight routinely make categorical distinctions between what they collectively sanction as "Hippie things" and what courses of action are to warrant their collective censure.

Consider, for example, the following field observations:

> I am talking with Ted, one of the Hip merchants, in his shop. Two other people, whom he occasionally employs, are present also, sporadically dipping into the conversation between Ted and myself when something sparks their interest. Ted identifies him-

self as a Hippie by all the usual indicators employed in the community (dress, beard, beads, drug use, Eastern philosophy, and proclaimed allegiance to "What the Hippies stand for"). I have never heard other members of the community deny him his identification, although I have heard them refer to other Hip merchants as "not really being Hippies." Ted has told me on some earlier occasion that he only employs Hippies because it "brings him down" (depresses him) to work with "Straights." Thus, it seems safe to conclude that the other two are also Hippies.

Ted and I begin to talk about what makes the Hippies significant, valuable, important. Ted tells me essentially that Hippies respect the concept of "individuality"; they "treat people as human beings, not as stereotypes that they (people) are not." One of the others comes in in support of Ted's description of what Hippies believe in and do.

Eventually we move from the topic of Hippies to the topic of "tourists" (who constitute any non-member who comes to the District to view the scene, but who, presumably, doesn't believe in it). The "tourists" have been heavy on the street for the past few weeks and their presence has been a constant topic of conversation in the community in general. Ted tells me that the "tourists bring everybody down; they think the Haight is a zoo. They look at us like animals, not individuals. They're all uptight and they're trying to contaminate us too."

By now I am becoming a little annoyed; I've heard this general argument so many times. The gist of it is that the Hippies understand completely what the "tourist" is but the "tourist" can never understand what the Hippie is because the Hippie is a complete individual, unique, complex. I respond to Ted by saying, "Aren't you stereotyping the tourist?" He denies this adamantly. The other two support him fully. The discussion ends with the three of them, almost in unison, telling me that "Hippies do their own thing" and "Tourists are conformists."

One of the self-identified Diggers has announced at the Town Hall Meeting a few days before that he has attempted and apparently been successful in having the Grayline Tour Buses stop "bringing busloads of Straights through the community to stare at us like we were freaks and animals." His announcement evokes a good deal of pleasure and excitement on the part of about eighty or ninety Hippies present at the meeting. The rest of the Hippies also apparently agree with him that if outsiders want to come to the Haight, they should come on foot, mix with the Hippies. If outsiders do this, they cannot help but "feel the 'good vibrations' " that emanate from the District, and presumably, if they are not converted, at least they will enjoy the experience more.

Two days later I encounter on the street five Hippies whom I had seen at the meeting. They did not explicitly disagree with the Digger's announcement and so I presume they accept it. Certainly it was in general accordance with the Hippie ideology. The five Hippies are engaged in studiously performing for the numerous tourists who are walking down the street. Each time a group of tourists walk by them, one of the males begins to massage the breasts of one of the females, while a second male calls out to the tourists, "Hey, watch this!" and the rest of the group stare openly at the tourists' embarrassment and discomfort.

It is a warm Sunday afternoon. Haight Street is crowded with clusters of Hippies, sitting in the doorways of the shops, sitting and lying against the front of the shops, lounging against the parked cars, and idly milling up and down the street. There are not too many tourists on the street today, but one comes along, complete with two cameras slung over his shoulder. The tourist has a look of somewhat startled pleasure on his face: he is smiling, apparently enjoying himself, and seemingly appreciating what he sees.

The tourist approaches a cluster of Hippies lounging against one of the cars. Only a few minutes earlier, I had been listening to their conversation, which was essentially that love would set the "Straight" world straight. The tourist, with deference and politeness, requests permission from the Hippies to take their photograph. One of the Hippies says to him, "I'd like to take that camera and bash it in your face." Two or three other Hippies nod in apparent agreement; none of them protest the response.

Clearly, "tourists" in the Haight are not to be considered by the Hippies as "someone just doing his own thing"; nor are Hippies whose slogan is "love" to be censured for any displays of animosity which they make toward "tourists."

So let us consider what the Hippies of the Haight collectively do treat as sanctioned everyday activities, as embodying the *social meaning* of their ideological maxims. In this sense, we may conceptualize their sanctioned social practices as conduct which falls within the realm of what members understand the moral maxims to be asserting all along and in the first place. In the following chapters, I shall focus on the characteristic formulation of those routine courses of action. The problem to be addressed in each of these chapters is: *Given the routine formulation of those courses of action, what considerations must be brought to bear by the members if their action is to be treated as congruent with what the ideology implies.*

Again, it must be clear that these chapters, taken together, do not exhaust the culture of the Hippies of the Haight, either necessarily in terms of beliefs or actually in terms of practices. My intent is only to describe the links between elements of the culture by demonstrating the reasonable paths of social inference which can exist for members of the culture. Thus, the claim for the validity of the ideology presented above does not rest on how many Hippies believe a little, somewhat, or very much of the ideology; for showing that more Hippies believe in visions than don't, does not validate the vision as a feature of the Hippie ideology. Instead it is assumed that it is sufficient to describe the fact that Hippies talk to one another (and sometimes address the general public) about visions as an existing social fact. This observation serves to specify "visions" as a feature of the Hippie ideology. The accompanying discussion of "visions" is meant only to describe the generally understood referent of the term as it is used by the Hippies of the Haight.

## NOTES

1. For an explicit discussion of this general problem in sociological analysis, see "On the Interpretation of Weltanschauung," in Karl Mannheim, *Essays on the Sociology of Knowledge* (London: Routledge and Kegan Paul, 1959), pp. 33–83. The problem is formally the same as that posed by Max Weber with respect to the analytic con-

struction of ideal types in *The Methodology of the Social Sciences* (Glencoe, Ill.: The Free Press, 1949), and by George Simmel with respect to the analysis of the forms of social life in *The Sociology of George Simmel* (Glencoe, Ill.: The Free Press, 1950).

2. Cf. Garfinkel, *Studies in Ethnomethodology* (Englewood Cliffs, N.J.: Prentice Hall, 1967).

3. Cf. Karl Mannheim, *Ideology and Utopia* (New York: Harcourt, Brace and Co., 1936), p. 59, Bronislaw Malinowski, *Magic, Science and Religion* (Garden City, N.Y.: Doubleday Anchor, 1955), particularly pp. 237–254, and David Mandelbaum, "The World and the World View of the Kota," in Y. Cohen, ed., *Social Structure and Personality* (New York: Holt, Rinehart, and Winston, 1961), pp. 288–309.

4. Aaron Cicourel, *Method and Measurement in Sociology* (London: Collier-Macmillan, 1964), pp. 189–224, and *The Social Organization of Juvenile Justice* (New York: John Wiley and Sons, 1968), pp. 1–21, as well as Ward Goodenough, "Cultural Anthropology and Linguistics," in Dell Hymes, ed., *Language in Culture and Society* (New York: Harper and Row, 1964), pp. 36–39.

5. Cf. Godfrey and Monica Wilson, *The Analysis of Social Change* (Cambridge: Cambridge University Press, 1954), p. 68.

6. Leonard Wolf, *Voices of the Love Generation* (Boston: Little, Brown and Co., 1968).

7. See Sheldon Messinger, "Life as Theater," *Sociometry*, Vol. 25 (1962), pp. 98–110.

8. The role of the supernatural vision as the basis for belief systems is similarly noted in Weston LaBarre, "Primitive Psychotherapy in Native American Cultures: Peyotism and Confession," *J. of Abn. and Soc. Psych.*, Vol. 42 (1947), pp. 294–308.

9. The beliefs about drugs, as they are related to the ideology in general, will be addressed in Chap. 6.

10. Wolf, *op. cit.*, pp. 197–198.

11. *Ibid.*, pp. 114, 139.

12. Cf. Ludwig Wittgenstein, *Tractatus Logic-Philosophicus* (London: Routledge and Kegan Paul, 1961), p. 7.

13. Wolf, *op. cit.*, pp. 207–208.

14. *Ibid.*, pp. 122–123.

15. The importance of the role of the guru is essentially in this context: the guru teaches by example, structuring the situation so that the student will thus learn on his own whatever there is for him to learn.

16. Wolf, *op. cit.,* p. 175.

17. Time is in effect foreshortened. In contrast with the conventional formulation of time, primary emphasis is placed on "now"—the immediately present moment. The role of time per se will be addressed in Chapter 5.

18. Wolf, *op. cit.,* p. 28.

19. *Ibid.,* p. 10.

20. *Ibid.,* p. 220.

21. *Ibid.,* p. 89.

22. Cf. Emile Durkheim, *The Division of Labor in Society* (Glencoe, Ill.: The Free Press, 1960), on mechanical and organic solidarity, and Karl Mannheim, *Essays on the Sociology of Knowledge, op. cit.,* on the social distribution of knowledge.

23. Wolf, *op. cit.,* p. 32.

24. For a discussion of the locating of individuals in terms of segments of their lives socially shared with others, see George Simmel, *op. cit.,* pp. 26–39.

25. In somewhat different terms, the community is not composed of individual-man-in-relationship-to-individual-man, but of men's-consciousness-in-relationship-to-men's-physical-conditions.

26. From Steve Levine, "Fifth Song," *San Francisco Oracle,* February, 1967.

27. Wolf, *op. cit.,* p. 161.

28. *Ibid.,* p. 55.

29. *Ibid.,* pp. 139–140.

30. Gilbert Ryle, "Categories," in A. Flew, ed., *Logic and Language* (Garden City, N.Y.: Doubleday Anchor), pp. 281–298.

31. Garfinkel, *op. cit.,* pp. 13, 34. See also, E. O. Arewa and Alan Dundes, "Proverbs and the Ethnography of Speaking Folklore," *Ethnography of Communication, American Anthropologist,* Vol. 66, pt. 2 (1964), pp. 70–85.

32. Garfinkel, *op. cit.,* pp. 76–115.

33. *Ibid.*

34. See George Miller, Eugene Galenter, and Karl Pribram, *Plans and the Structure of Behavior* (New York: Holt, Rinehart, and Winston, 1960).

35. Cf. Wolf, *ibid.*

# Part Three

# AN EXAMINATION
# OF THE PROBLEM

In addressing the relationship between beliefs and practices, I have formulated the sociological problem as one in which *beliefs* may be thought of as roughly the independent variable; *practices* the dependent variable. The intervening or explanatory variable is that of *ideological interpretations*. Following Goodenough, Frake, and others,[1] I shall treat the terms of the language which the Hippies of the Haight routinely employ as matters which have, for them, both ideological and practical significance.

When anyone with an ordinary comprehension of the Orthodox American language (the language as it is conventionally spoken) listens to the speech of the Hippies of the Haight, a number of linguistic terms stand out as *particular* to the language of *this* group. Among those terms are words such as "straight," "groovy," "hassle," "happening," "trip toy," "just being," "rapping," "scarfing," and "dealing." Such terms are routinely employed by members during the ongoing course of their everyday life to provide answers to very general questions, such as "What is this?" "What are you doing?" "What is happening?"

Let us consider the argot of the Hippies as characterizing

features of the world that are distinctive for members of the group. That is, let us treat the terms of the argot as *objectifying* the differences between the Hippie community and the conventional community. As such, the argot terms can stand as indicators of socially significant features of the Hippie world.

In addressing matters of actual practice in this way, it is assumed that the language used by a group can be employed as a starting point to investigate the properties of the world that are socially significant to the members of that group.[2] The empirical referent can then be specified for any given term by describing actual matters of conduct that the members typically mean (i.e., refer to) when they use such words. These actual matters of conduct are thus to be conceptualized as the "practical significance" of the terms. At the same time, for each array of "practical significance" associated with a given term, there should be an array of "ideological significance" which members treat as "corresponding to" or "justifying" those actual patterns of conduct.

## NOTES

1. Ward Goodenough, "Culture Anthropology and Linguistics," in D. Hymes, ed., *Language, Culture and Society* (New York: Harper and Row, 1964), pp. 36–39. Charles Frake, "How to Ask for a Drink in Subanun," *American Anthropology*, Vol. 66, pt. 2 (1964), pp. 127–132.

2. For similar use of this general methodological procedure, see Gresham M. Sykes, *Society of Captives* (New York: Atheneum, 1965), David Maurer, *The Big Can* (New York: Signet Books, 1962), and David Maurer, *The Whiz Mob* (New Haven, Conn.: College and University Press, 1964).

# 5

## Doing Everyday Hippie Things

The Hippie community exists in calendar time as a group of people who individually identify themselves as Hippies. They are also located in a particular district; and they are engaged in doing what *they* collectively recognize as "everyday Hippie things," either alone or with others.

The Hippie as a flesh-and-blood person, viewing his circumstances within the context of his culture, embarks on courses of *social* action: conduct that is guided in its course by the corresponding meaning attributed to it. The source of that meaning is to be found in the individual's own practical understanding of what he, as a member, believes. His knowledge of the Hippie ideology thus serves as a matter of practical knowledge in a variety of ways. A member may employ it as a standard of judgment to evaluate his present situation; he may use it as a method for assessing the motive and character of others; he may take it into consideration in formulating his own courses of action; he may invoke it to define his situation; he may acknowledge it to explain whatever needs explaining.

## CALENDRICAL DAYS

Between "getting out of bed" and "getting into bed," a "typical" day in the Hippie community may include such activities as dressing, eating, working, just being, being with others, and happenings. It may include any or all of these events, for in terms of the ideology of the Hippies of the Haight, today is simply given. Reality as they formulate it is the present now and it requires no operational indices (as the occurence of some particular event) to know that it is. What one does in fact do in a typical day is almost (but as I will point out below, not quite) a matter of personal preference: a matter of psychic whim.[1]

Thus, while a typical day begins with waking, in the Hippie community one need not get out of bed for the day to stlll constitute a "typical day." This perspective is exemplified in the following illustrations:

> I ask Linda what she did yesterday and she replies, "I stayed in bed and blew grass." I respond, "Really?" with a tone of amazement in my voice and she replies rather flatly, "I do that sometimes."

> One of the males in the apartment mentions to Don that he slept "all day yesterday." On the "yesterday" in question there was a large happening in the park that the rest of the group has been reminiscing about. But Don apparently doesn't find it strange that the other slept all day. I ask Don after we leave the apartment whether, by sleeping all day, the other fellow has "missed anything." Don does not seem to understand what I am talking about. I get the feeling I have made an irrelevant remark.

### *1. Dressing*

"Dressing" constitutes an activity for the Hippies of the Haight when one selects something to embellish one's body out of what there is available. Dressing thus constitutes purposeful activity, but its goal is not to "make oneself socially presentable." Rather one dresses to "make oneself beautiful," to feel good personally.

One can do this upon getting out of bed; or one can do this anytime during the course of the day that it seems desirable.[2] No reason need be perceivable to others, (as the first field observation below indicates) and no grounds exist for others to question the sense of the activity (as indicated by the second field observation).

> Stella has been playing the piano in the men's long underwear (that I think, but am not certain, she usually sleeps in). She ends one selection, sits for a moment in a meditative posture at the piano, and then goes into the other room. When she comes back she is now wearing a skirt with a woven Indian design on it and a blouse of indeterminate origin. She sits down at the piano and continues to play.

> Four of us have gathered in Marie's apartment. We are planning to go to a party up the street. Guy and Nora decide to "turn on" first, and so the rest of us just sit, waiting. Eventually, Guy's girl friend stands up and says, "Let's go" and the rest begin preparations to leave: putting the grass away, blowing out the candles, turning off the record player, and finally getting their coats and turning out the lights. When the five of us are on the street outside, Mark suddenly announces he "wants to get dressed" and he goes back into the apartment. Nobody says anything about it. We just stand outside talking until he comes back and then we go on to the party. Mark originally had on one brightly colored pair of pants and shirt and a heavy blue jacket. He now has on another pair of brightly colored pants, paisley shirt, and the same blue jacket.

## 2. Eating

The ingestion of food among Hippies of the Haight routinely incorporates two varieties of "eating." One variety is what might be called "just eating." I found no special linguistic way to refer to "just eating." This activity takes place on any occasion when members of the Hippie community eat conventional food. The activity may include eating two or three separate, prepared courses, and the specific foods so included may, and frequently do, parallel conventional meals. Such "just eating" is an "everyday Hippie thing," although what and when one eats are left open to individual preference.

The following part of an interview from *Voices of the Love Generation* provides a typical example:

> "So I woke up this morning and I made a book cover for my *Scheherazade* book out of jungle material. I sewed it and made it really beautiful. And then Sandra had some pea soup cookin'— split pea soup with carrots in it—and we brought it in with some tea—it was around eleven o'clock, I guess . . . I ate breakfast of my split pea soup in a glass. I really enjoyed it." [3]

However, a typical Hippie day may, and quite likely will, include what is sometimes referred to as "scarffing" and sometimes heard referred to as "eating head food." "Scarffing" is known to the members as taking place whenever it is that one eats specifiable foods that are considered, by the members of the Hippie community, to be particularly delectable when one is "high" on drugs. Two such "scarffing" foods are ice cream and peanut butter, but the general list is rather extensive and always considered open to the discovery of new additions.

The following excerpts from field notes provide two examples:

> David, William, and Iris have all been smoking grass. We are in the car, on our way to Marin County. We have been driving about fifteen minutes when David notices a small grocery store and says, "Let's get something to eat." We stop; David and William go into the store and then return with a large brown paper sack. They get back in the car and David announces, "I have decided what we need is a three-course dinner." He then opens the sack and, along with William, begins to laugh even before Iris and I can see what it contains. The joke is presumably calling it a "three-course-dinner" since what there is consists of four ice cream sandwiches, four candy bars, and a box of chocolate-covered donuts—all considered to be "good head foods."

> Ed is standing at the counter of the coffee house, eating one of the cookies from the bin while he is waiting for his order (a

pastrami sandwich). He brings it to the table where Hank and I are sitting, eats it, and then goes back, to return with a piece of Baklava. A little while later he surreptitiously takes a jar of jam and a spoon off the counter and consumes virtually all the jam that was left in the jar (about a third). Hank says to me, as the two of us watch Ed, "I really enjoy watching Ed eat when he's high."

Members of the Hippie community frequently see the "scarffing" of others as a sign that they are high on drugs. They do not need to know whether others have been "using drugs" since "scarffing" is treated as a "natural" sign of being "high." An example is provided by the following field observations:

> Harvey and I are walking along Haight Street. It seems extraordinarily crowded, and there are a large number of relatively young-looking people. Harvey points out to me how many people are eating ice cream—a substantial proportion of those on the street. He then goes on to say, "Everybody on the street is high tonight."

Since "using drugs" may take place at any time, "scarffing" may be observed any time as well. For example, in one of the corner stores in the District I have encountered Hippies purchasing ice cream, Dolly Madison cakes, and other "head food" as early as 9 A.M., when the store opens. Furthermore, members' recognition of the relationship between "what one is eating or preparing to eat" and "being high" is often mutually acknowledged. In the grocery store, any indication on my part of noting the particular purchases they are making (even where we are not previously acquainted) usually evokes a smile in response, presumably in recognition of the fact that I have recognized their state.[4]

## 3. Working

For members of the Hippie community who work either sporadically or regularly, conditions of employment serve to limit the freedom of choice they can have in deciding what to do at any given moment. Working thus links them into the conventional temporal order of things.

If we consider "working" as any instance of remunerative activity in which members of the Hippie community engage, there are various forms of this activity which can be discerned. Some of these forms are more conventionally delimited than others. As a result, the extent of personal preference that can be brought into play with respect to working is itself variable: the less conventional the form of employment the less stringent the links to the conventional temporal order.

The community ideal is the "independent craftsman." In part, the value of this occupational category rests on the fact that the concept of the craftsman implies someone actively engaged in the full production of whatever he is doing and hence someone who is free from "arbitrary" structuring of his activity, and "in harmony" with his total environment.[5] The following field excerpts exemplify this part of the ideal of the independent craftsman:

> Hank has dropped by to give me a drawing he has done. In the course of conversation he mentions that he has been taken on as an apprentice, to learn the art of stone engraving and printing. He says that he is very pleased because "it's much better than steel engraving—stone is a part of nature." He continues, mentioning that it is also much more difficult, that it requires "all of you to do it, not just your hands but your whole arms and body."

> I am arguing with one of the Hip craftsmen about some work I brought to him. I had told him exactly what I had wanted done when I brought it in. He had not done it that way and I am not pleased with the way he has done it. To my anger he replies, "I did it this way because it was the right way to do it. I knew what I was doing." He continues with a long discourse on the difference between someone who "just works" and "a craftsman"; the former does anything for money; the latter does only what he knows should be done.

> (For about three months after this incident, each time I encounter him he continues to bring up the matter by reiterating what I had asked him to do and why he decided to do it the way he did.)

But it is equally important that the *independent* craftsman (as opposed to the craftsman-as-entrepreneur) is free to work or not as a matter predicated solely on personal preference. Thus, upon occasion, Hippies interested in and capable of doing jewelry and leather work have mentioned that they "don't want to hassle" with having a shop—the referent of "hassle" being the commitment to working, regardless of whether they feel like it or not.

For such independent craftsmen, remuneration depends on finding some outlet for their product. Many of the Hip shops along the street take in handicraft articles on a consignment basis (as do some non-Hip stores outside the District). Another outlet is individual referrals of potential "customers" to the craftsmen, as the following field excerpt notes:

> Susan has introduced me to a friend, Runee, whom she says "makes very fine jewelry." The three of us talk about jewelry-making in general, and I ask Runee whether the jewelry he makes is placed in the shops on the street on consignment. He says no, that "people know I make good jewelry and they know where to find me, so if they come to me and want to buy it, I sell it to them." I go on to say that such an arrangement sounds like it would lead to a very erratic source of income. Runee replies that he would rather have an erratic source of income than "hassle" with the merchants (of the Hip stores).

A necessary aspect of independent craftsmanship is that no deadlines for completion dates will be set. It seems to be generally understood that when a buyer commissions an independent crafts-man to make some particular article, the price may be settled in advance, but the time of completion is to be left as a matter to be decided by the craftsman himself. Thus, on one occasion, in talking to a craftsman with a sandal shop on the street, I mentioned that I had a friend who did leather work and was planning to have him make some sandals. The reply to my remark was "If you want to know when they'll be done you ought to let me make them for you." On another occasion, visiting a jewelry maker, I noted that a necklace he began making on commission almost two months earlier was still on his bench. He said simply, "I'm not done with it yet."

Finally, independent craftsmen can at any time take their wares and peddle them directly on the street, both to other members of the community and to tourists. This alternative is accepted as routine. Such direct selling requires no particular planning, as the following field note illustrates.

> Stan has come over and we have been sitting around the kitchen table, just chatting. At one point he takes some brightly colored wool out of his pocket and asks if there are any sticks around. Somebody gets up and comes back with a few. Stan idly starts making God's Eyes, although he continues to participate in the sporadic conversation. He makes three of them, and then stops, leaving them in the middle of the table. About a half-hour later he suddenly announces "I think I'll take these (the God's Eyes) up to Haight (Street) and sell them." He and Carol, who has decided to go with him, leave.
>
> (A few days later I ask Carol if Stan sold the God's Eyes when they went to Haight Street and she says no.)

To some extent, the Hip entrepreneurs (whether they are craftsmen or simply merchants) are committeed to a more regular pattern of work, although the regularity is not necessarily the same as it is in more conventional establishments. Thus, while some of the shops along Haight Street are consistently open on certain days and during specifiable hours, others are much more sporadic. This latter pattern appears from the following excerpts of conversation with one of the Hip merchants on the street.

> Ted has the days and hours that his shop is open placed on the door, although on a number of occasions when I have dropped by to see him during these times the shop has been closed. Sometimes when the shop is closed there will be a note on the door indicating when he will be back. I have encountered him at the coffee house during the hours he has posted as being "open for business," and mentioned that I came by the other day and he was closed; and that I came back when the note on the door said he would be back and he was still closed. He answers, to my implicit rebuke, "That's why I have my shop on Haight Street instead of

someplace else. I could probably make more money someplace else, but there would be no satisfaction in it."

He goes on to say that the reason he "dropped out" of the Conventional society was the lack of freedom he had, that before he came to Haight Street he was "doing the same thing I am now, only then I had to do it even when I didn't want to."

The preferential options for Hip entrepreneurs include not only when they will be open for business but what will take place in their establishment while they are open for business. Many of the Hip shops along the street, which are open ostensibly for the sale of merchandise, are used by members of the community as informal gathering places. It appears to be mutually understood by both the merchants and the members of the community that such use of the establishments is sanctioned.[6]

In the same sense, for those who are ostensibly working in such establishments, attending to business need not be granted priority over other activities. Consider the following two field observations: [7]

I have been standing, talking with Ted in his shop for twenty minutes. During this time no potential customers have come in. At one point Ted is explaining something to me about the Hippie community, and another Hippie comes in. The potential customer stands a few feet away from us, apparently waiting for an opportunity to request something of Ted. However, Ted ignores him, even when he asks "Is there anyone working here?" After his potential customer leaves, and when I get an opportunity, I ask Ted why he didn't help him. Ted replies, "Because I was talking to you."

I have been talking to the entrepreneurs of one of the Hip shops and some of the customers lounging around in the establishment. Bruce, one of the customers, says he has some business to take care of with some Hippie entrepreneurs outside the District and asks if I have a car and could give him a ride. I agree, and on the way we drop off one of the others who had been talking with us and who decided to go home.

When we reach the office there is a girl sitting at a desk, typing. She tells Bruce that the person he wants to see is not there right now but will return "very soon." Bruce says he will wait, and we sit down on the couch. The girl continues typing, occasionally answering the phone, in response to what sound like business calls. Bruce and I talk for a while, and the "secretary" (as she appears to be) eventually asks if we'd like to listen to some music. She puts a Beatles record on, quite loud, and then goes back to her typing. By now two other Hippies have wandered in, sit on the floor, and listen to the music. During this time, the "secretary" has also been smoking a joint. She eventually brings out some loose grass and some papers, suggesting that anyone who wants one is welcome to roll his own. Bruce and one of the other Hippies who have come in do so; the third says "I'm so high on acid . . ." (the implication being nothing more is needed).

I sit around for almost an hour with Bruce before I have to leave. During this time the "secretary" has brought out some cookies, changed the record on the request of one of the others there, and continued with her typing and answering the telephone.

For some Hippies, working consists of being salaried by Hip merchants or selling Hip merchandise on commission. The latter pattern is most frequently observed in the hawking of various Underground newspapers through the District. Newspaper hawking in the District provides the most desirable form of working for those who are neither craftsmen nor entrepreneurs, and yet are not willing to be bound by conventional obligations in order to obtain any remuneration from their activity. The newspapers are distributed to sellers at various locations. Once they have claimed their stock, the sellers are free to sell as many or as few as they want, and to sell them whenever they desire. Since the papers come out only once a week (and sometimes less often) the temporal demands for work are minimal. I have occasionally encountered newspaper sellers selling issues which are no longer current, particularly to tourists. However, they will also offer outdated papers to members of the community as well. In one instance, when I asked about it, the seller replied, "If you haven't read it already, it doesn't matter what the date is."

Occasionally, Hippies employed in Hip establishments in the District will complain that their Hip employers are as demanding as any conventional merchant. But for the most part, (at least as the matter has arisen in casual conversation among members) the prevalent opinion seems to be that, if one must be salaried, it is preferable to be salaried within the community itself, since, as they say, "It's not so uptight-business here."

Similarly, the Job-Co-op that was established in the District provides opportunity for what is characteristically occasional work, e.g., baby sitting, handyman work, and other odd jobs. The Job-Co-op sometimes gives the impression of a union hall, with members waiting inside for jobs to appear. Yet on the occasions I talked with Hippies waiting around inside the office, there are often more who are there "just being" and "being social" than are there "looking for work." Those with whom I have spoken who have used the Job-Co-op to get work characteristically mention that its primary advantage is that "you only have to work when you want to."

Conventional positions are filled by working Hippies. For many, the Post Office is considered the most desirable job, though not merely because such jobs are easily obtainable.[8] The pay is relatively good, but for those who are delivering the mail there is also considerable on-the-job discretion in how the work is to be managed. The following comments from members employed at one time or another by the Post Office are indicative of this aspect of the job.[9]

> "When you deliver mail you can be outside. And most of all there's nobody standing there telling you which side of the street to go on. And if you want to, you don't even have to go to this house right after you go to that house."

> "I have a route and I deliver the mail on it. When I want to and how I want to."

The same perspective can be found in conversation with one member about why she turned down a job at the Post Office after it was offered to her. She said:

> "They assigned me to work at Rincon [the main mail handling

annex in the city]. I wanted to deliver mail. If you work at Rincon, all you do is act like a big machine: put this letter in that slot, carry this package to that desk—march . . ."

However, many members of the community do work *in* the Post Office as well as *for* the Post Office. Particularly on the night shift at Rincon Annex, from indices such as the apparel of the employees, one gets the impression that one has not left the Haight.

Other Hippies work in various types of conventional jobs that in various ways set standard, conventional restraints on the daily round of activity of members. The personal attitudes of such members toward their work may be variable. Some accept it as "normal trouble" and for the most part say nothing particular about it.[10]

As the following field observations indicate, Hippies may be quite casual about their occupations or any particular conventional employment slot at any particular time.

> I encounter Frances on the street, greet her, and then remark that I thought she would be at work today. She replies, in a very matter of fact tone, "I didn't feel like it."

> Five of us are sitting around Sandy's apartment. Leon says he is looking for a job. Sandy says that Leon had just gotten a job two days ago. Leon replies, "I quit. I didn't like it."

> Tony is telling me that he is going to quit his job which he has been working at for more than seven months. I ask him why, saying that I thought he enjoyed what he was doing. He replies, "I don't think I do any more. Too much hassle." (He quit three days later.)

> Nora has had the same job for better than a year, and on one or two occasions in the past had mentioned to me that that has been the longest period of time she has stayed on one job. This evening, however, she says, "I told them at work I was going to quit in two weeks, so they better look for a replacement." I ask why, mentioning her previous remarks about the fact that she has stayed there longer than she had stayed at jobs in

the past. Her reply was essentially that that was *just* why she was quitting now.

At the same time, just as members may take the job they are working at casually, they may also take it seriously. All one needs to do is claim that one's job is one's "thing" to provide the justification for meeting whatever temporal demands that job requires. Thus, on occasions when members have asked me why I work and I reply that I work because I enjoy what I'm doing, my response will frequently evoke comments such as "That's good. I wish I had a job like that." Presumably, "like that" does not refer to the particular kind of work I do, but to the fact that I am doing what I like to do.

## 4. Just Being

For the Hippies of the Haight, "just being" is a sanctioned residual category of behavior similar to the conventional category of "just busy." Activity contained within the category is anything that members can properly do. But those activities do not have a specific linguistic designation or definable boundaries which might separate one instance of the category of "just being" from another.[11]

The following field excerpts provide three examples of how members describe the "activity" of just being:

Walt and I encounter John on the street. Walt and John know one another, but the latter has not been in the city for two or three months. Walt inquires about when John returned and then asks him what he has been doing since he returned. John responds, "Oh, just being." Walt nods, and as we start to part, Walt says to John, "Why don't you come over to my place if you get a chance?"

Tony has quit his job about four weeks ago. At the time he quit I asked him what he was planning to do and he answered that he didn't know. I have seen him occasionally in the park since then but have not spoken to him. He is at Nora's apartment this evening and I ask him what he has been doing since he quit his job. Tony answers, "Just being, but I've decided to do some leatherwork now."

I have been sitting on the grass in the Panhandle by myself. There are no more than twenty-five or thirty Hippies in the park today, most of them in groups of three or four. Someone I have never seen before stops by where I am sitting and says to me, "Just being?" I look up at him, and before I can say anything, he smiles and continues on.

In the course of "just being" members in effect meander through the day, caught up in no particular thing and in company of no particular person. "Just being" may be collective, as it is frequently observed on the street and in the park; or it may be individual.

Since my very presence as an observer would serve to create a situation where acknowledgement that I am "with" members can occur, my direct observations of "just being" are for the most part observations from the street and the parks.

The following field notes provide two descriptions of Hippies collectively engaged in "just being."

This is the second occasion where a rock band has come to the Panhandle to form the nucleus of a happening. A large number of Hippies encircle the truck bed (used as a stage), as well as a number of people who, at least from their dress, do not appear to be members of the Hippie community. The group in the immediate vicinity of the music is tightly packed. There is a small open area where some are dancing, and the others are for the most part focusing on either the band or the dancers, if they can see them.

An equally large number of Hippies are scattered around the grassy slopes in groups of varying sizes. There is some conversation within these groups, as well as some interchange on the part of others who are walking around through the park. Those walking, either singly or with one or two others, will stop momentarily, engage in conversation with those sitting, and then walk on or sit and join those they have spoken to for a while. A substantial number of Hippies, however, both sitting and walking, appear to be alone. Examples of what they are doing are:

1) sitting with their eyes closed and their heads tilted up toward the rather weak sun
2) sitting with legs crossed, staring into the middle distance between their heads and their knees
3) lying on their stomachs, plucking idly at the grass
4) walking slowly along the asphalt paths, with their eyes apparently focused on the toes of their feet
5) inspecting the shrubbery

Of those I have seen so "engaged," there is also one male stringing some fine glass beads and a girl walking along, tinkling a mass of brass bells on her hands and arms, watching them quite intently. I try to keep track of five or six of them. Of the ones walking, none engage anyone else in conversation while I can see them. Three remain sitting for almost an hour.

Sunday on Haight Street: generally crowded with Hippies lining both sides of the pavement and meandering down the sidewalk. The usual clusters of tourists are present. East of Masonic, the street is not as crowded. Outside of one of the coffee houses a cluster of Hippies is engaged in animated conversation. Around them, mainly sitting on the doorsteps, are a number of inanimate Hippies. One is making a God's Eye, the others are just sitting.

Further up the street there are a few others just sitting on some available doorsteps. One male is leaning up against the rear of a parked car, his back arched, his face toward the sky, his arms outstretched. I stand and watch him for about ten minutes, but he doesn't move.

In the large back room of one of the Hippie shops a rock group is sporadically practicing, although they play no one number completely through and there are periods of silence between their music which stretch on to almost forty-five minutes. There are a large number of Hippies in the back room as well. Some wander in, look around, listen to the music for a while, and then go out. Many of them are sitting with their backs up against the walls, silently, with their heads either back against the wall or bowed toward their chests. Unlike the ones who walk in and then walk out, those sitting do little, if any, looking around the room. Some of those sitting, who were there when I came, are still sitting when I leave after almost two hours.

## 5. Being Social

"Being social" in the Hippie community refers to any encounter of two or more members where, at some point or other, there is mutual acknowledgement of a co-presence. Thus, the distinction between "being social" and "just being" rests not on the particular substantive activity that is taking place, but only on the mutual recognition that there is more than one person "present."

One of the most usual forms that "being social" takes among the Hippies of the Haight is talking. Talking is not the only form of being social,[12] but the structure of this activity in the Hippie community has a particular interest. It tends to exemplify what might be called the members' creation of structure in terms of simultaneity.

Talking within the Hippie community takes place in two ways. In one, what the members call "rapping" usually involves the extended remarks of a speaker focused on some particular topic, or related topical issues. "Rapping" is thus, to the Hippies of the Haight, the equivalent of carrying on an extended discourse in the conventional society, even though here it has an indigenous term.[13] However, "rapping" is somewhat different from conventional discourse in that it does not require more than one vocal participant. Further, it does not require other participants to respond directly. Finally, it does not require other participants even to acknowledge that it has taken place. The following provides a typical example of some of these aspects of "rapping":

> Craig has continued for almost twenty minutes, talking about his family, his relationship with his family and the things that he particularly likes about them. During this time the three other people present have been quiet, but they have not (as far as I can tell) been paying any particular attention to him. Craig ends his discourse quite suddenly, (and he seems almost embarrassed), saying "Wow, I've really been rapping." Somebody else then says something about getting something to eat and the group disperses.

"Rapping" may take place between two or more people as

well. Hippies of the Haight, however, use the term "rapping" to describe only those occasions where the extended exchange of remarks between participants is focused on some identifiable topic (or set of interrelated topics) and where those exchanges are not interspersed with any noticeable exchange of remarks on non-related topics. For the members of the Hippie community, then, "rapping" is the equivalent of what is considered in the conventional society "a recognizable discourse about something." The following excerpt from field observations exemplifies this aspect of "rapping":

> There are about eight people in the room. They are watching television, but the volume of the television set is off and the radio has been turned on rather loudly. Occasionally remarks are exchanged between two people about various things, and occasionally someone will make a comment to the group at large about the visual events on the television screen. A commercial comes on that seems to catch everyone's attention. Beth makes some remark about it and then Brian says, "Hey, turn it up. I want to hear what it [the commercial] is rapping about."

Further, "rapping" is almost always labeled as such or called to attention, whenever it occurs. It stands, in this sense, as a notable event for members, on the basis of its perceived "strangeness." "Rapping" occurs outside of the ideological framework of the community. One would thus assume that members can "rap" only because they are knowledgeable about a world in which the form of "rapping" is sensible (i.e., the conventional social world from which they all originally came). When they employ this form within their own world, it seems strange.[14]

For the members of the Hippie community the more sanctioned form of verbal activity is what may be considered "talking as usual." "Talking as usual" is constituted as a set of remarks which only afterwards may be rearranged as *interrelated* assertions about one or more particular topics. Members "having a conversation about something" is not a structural requirement for engaging in verbal activity. They may "talk about something" in the course of talking, but that "talk about something" is not necessarily separate and distinct; rather it is interspersed within other ongoing verbal activity.[15]

Excerpts from field notes of my own attempts to "coherently describe" the verbal activity going on provide an example of what stands for the Hippies of the Haight as "talking as usual."

Ray, Felix, another male, and myself are at a table in the coffee house. Ray and Felix have been talking about "finding" their respective selves. Felix suddenly says to me that he hasn't seen me around for a while and I reply that I have been out of town. Felix asks where I have been and I say, "Santa Barbara," and then go on and talk a little about the beach there. During this time, Ray and the other male have started talking about painting. A fourth male comes up to the table, greets Ray and Felix, and the three of them say something about a mutual acquaintance. The fourth male leaves and Ray and Felix continue talking about "finding" themselves.

Four of us are in the car, driving back to the city. David and William are carrying on a conversation about some "poor" quality acid William recently bought. David says that William has been "burned" (cheated) and he should try to get his money back. William wants to know if it is possible to get his money back; David says he should at least try. This entire conversation between David and William is fragmented and interspersed between:

1) passing remarks between David and Iris about someone the two of them know
2) David ruminating on the people who broke into his place in the country
3) William asking me about teaching at SF State
4) periods of complete silence
5) David and William talking about acid trips in general

I am at Gene's apartment, watching television with him and his wife Linda. During one period, the ongoing verbal output looks like the following:

1) Gene makes a remark about the TV program
2) Linda makes a remark about looking for a new apartment
3) Gene makes a remark about somebody who might know

of an apartment. (This seems to be a response of Gene to Linda's remark above)

4) Linda says something about the group that will be playing at the Fillmore Auditorium this weekend

5) Gene makes a remark about the TV program

6) Linda gives a very long account of a "vision" of a house she had when she was walking along the street yesterday

7) I make a remark about mysticism (in response to Linda's previous remark)

8) Gene says something about the Fillmore Auditorium. (this sounds like it might be a response to Linda's remark #4 above, but I'm not sure, since Linda had been talking about the group which would be playing and Gene is now talking about another group)

9) I say something about music to Gene (mainly as an attempt to find out what exactly is being talked about with respect to the Fillmore)

10) Linda begins to talk again about the same "vision" (cf remark #6 although what she now says sounds like a response to my remark #7)

Members can and do engage in conventionally structured conversations. They can also accept verbal activity which has no perceptible structure as a comprehensible course of action. Such activity is comprehensible given the ontological beliefs of members of the Hippie community. These beliefs postulate a world as simply a "given reality" where any linear sequence can be considered "arbitrarily" superimposed upon that world. Therefore, ongoing verbal utterances can be treated as just that. There is no requirement that any discernible meaning (in the sense of some shared perceivably similar referent) be clearly established. Rather, utterances can be simply treated as a kind of "music" emanating from the vocal apparatus of the speaker.[16] And this view is sanctioned.

If the speaker insists that the recipient treat his phonetic utterances seriously—take them as assertions with consequences to be acted upon subsequently—the recipient may respond with a sense of indignation.

I ran into Allen in the coffee house, sat down with him, and started telling him about some of the difficulties Mary and the others were experiencing at the meeting with the Straights. Mary had asked me to try to get as many Hippies to tomorrow's meeting as I could, and I agreed that I would. I went on for about five minutes, trying to explain the background of the problem to Allen and why it would be important for him to be at the meeting. Allen sat there listening to me, at first with an expression of presumed interest on his face, and then with an expression of confusion. When I was done he looked at me and said, "Man, what are you saying?"

I took his remark in a conventionally literal way, and began to recap what I had just said. Allen then said, "You're blowing my mind. I'm getting out of here," and in fact he got up and walked out of the coffee house.

Ongoing courses of action are like conversation or talking. They need not be structured in terms of some specific point or purpose, but rather are to be treated as simply "events that happen." And so, this expression of the ideological tenet of the world as given in the immediate present when put into practical action may result in what looks, from the perspective of non-members, like "aimless activity."

The following field observations provide three examples:

Ken and I are just getting into the car to go to the movies. Kathy comes out of the basement with a large drawstring bag in her arms. Neither Ken nor I have ever seen her before. She asks us if we will give her a ride to the laundromat and we agree. In the car she asks us where we are going and Ken says to the movies. Then he asks her if she wants to go. She agrees.

At the movies she disappears for almost an hour, then returns. She says nothing about leaving, and neither do we. Afterwards, we start to take her to her apartment on Haight Street. But when we are almost there she changes her mind and says she wants to go to the coffee house. So we drop her and her laundry bag off there.

Stella has been playing the piano in a pair of men's long underwear. At the same time Gene has been working on something he is making. Gene has had the radio on, tuned at a fairly loud volume. Eventually Stella stops playing the piano and starts doing

Yoga exercises in the middle of the room. Two males who have been staying in the apartment come in, stand and watch Stella for a while, and then go on into the back room without saying anything.

I have come by Brian's apartment unannounced. When I knock on his door, he calls to come in. Inside he has a large lens; underneath it there are bits of colored paper. The record player is on and Brian is rather abstractly dancing around the lens. Since he continues once I am in the room, without paying any further attention to me, I sit down and begin reading a book that I find next to the couch.

After about half an hour, Stan and another male walk in, glance at the two of us (Brian still abstractly dancing around the lens and me presumably reading). The other male joins Brian, and Stan sits down on the floor, staring up toward the ceiling. This goes on for a while until Brian finally stops circling around the lens and says, "Let's smoke some grass." At this point there is a sense of mutually focused action on the part of the three of them—at least for me as observer: Brian gets his stash, begins rolling a joint; Stan lights some sticks of incense; the other male begins looking through the stacks of records for one to put on the record player.

## 6. Happenings

For "a happening" to take place (for something to be recognized and named as a "happening" by the members of the Hippie community), it is not necessary that some number of previously disparate participants now engage in some mutually focused course of action. Rather, all that is required is that in some perceivably bounded area, disparate participants are simultaneously all caught up in *some* activity. When there is, in some specifiable area simultaneously music *and* dancing, *and* talking *and* admiring *and* singing *and* being, there is "a happening," regardless of how those activities may be distributed among the participants.

Dances are a characteristic instance of "happenings." Like the "happenings" in open public areas such as the streets and the parks, the dances take place in the various contained locales of the Hippie community (such as the auditoriums of the city which exist outside of the Haight-Ashbury District itself, but are treated by the Hippies of the Haight as a part of their territory) and are characterized by multifocused simultaneity.

Members of the Hippie community do not speak of "going to a dance"; but rather of "going to The Fillmore (auditorium)"; or "to the Avalon," to "The Straight Theater," "Winterland," or "The Longshoremen's." What can be done "at the Fillmore" is dancing, listening to music, watching the light show, concentrating on the strobe lights, seeing friends, meeting people, or just "having a groovy place for a trip" which is, by and large, a solitary activity of one's own psyche.

None of these discrete activities are unique to the Fillmore, or to any of the other auditoriums, although what is, for the members, special about the Fillmore or the other auditoriums is that all of these activities can be contained at the same time.

Hippies' sanctioned structuring of action in terms of simultaneity is of course notable in their form of dancing. Members' dancing has not infrequently been described by non-members as being "fragmented, disjointed, and unrelated movements" on the part of individuals acting individually. This description arises from employing the conventional understanding about how "dancing" will take place: as a reciprocally integrated interaction of movements on the part of two or more participants. However, as dancing is understood by members of the Hippie community, one can dance without first having found a partner, i.e., one can dance by one's self. And furthermore, as understood by the members of the Hippie community, one can dance without it having to be apparent *to others* that there is some "connection" between the movement of the dancer and the sounds of the music, i.e., one does not raise the question of "dancing" in tempo.

The following field observations of dances provide typical examples of this sense of structured simultaneity:

> Marion, her two children (aged five and seven), my son (aged seven), and I arrive at the Fillmore at around 9 P.M. There are about sixty or seventy people there already, many of them in

"high costume" although there are a good number in conventional dress. (Someone later tells me that many "straight kids" come to the dances, although he does not say why he thinks this is so. There are also a few sailors in uniform there.) When we arrive the music has not started, although there is a stationary light projection which covers the entire wall behind the musicians' stage and part of the ceiling as well. Most of the people are sitting and standing by the stage; the rest are dispersed over the dance floor (which is quite large) and scattered among the single row of seats that ring the dance floor. The general impression that I have at this point is one of simply "people milling, waiting for something to begin."

Eventually a few people start to "dance" (in the sense of two or three people standing in a somewhat cleared area of the floor and moving their bodies in some decisive way, unlike simply "wandering" around). This activity begins to spread through the group. By the time the musicians finally arrive, set up their electronic equipment, and begin to make music, there have been at least twenty-five or thirty people who have been dancing already.

The fluid light show (oil and water projections, taking place simultaneously with the running of film clips and the projection of various unrelated still pictures) begins at the same time the musicians begin. By now (about 10 P.M.) there must be at least two hundred or more people in the auditorium. Perhaps a half of them are dancing, the rest sitting, standing, and some lying, near the stage. Others are sitting in the seats ringing the floor and in the seats on the balcony.

Dancers get up singly, in twos, threes, and fours, coming into one another's vicinity and dispersing without any perceivable pattern. I ask Marion what the "name" of the dances they are doing are, but she shrugs and says "they are just dancing." I get the feeling that my request for the "name" of the dance makes no sense to her; has no relevance to what she understands is taking place. The children (ours as well as perhaps a dozen others, ranging in age from three to nine years) are exuberantly running about the dance floor, around, in between, and occasionally into the dancers, but nobody pays any attention to them. Somewhat later, a group of three elaborately costumed Hippies takes the hands of our three children and brings them into a circling, linked movement. But within a few minutes the children have apparently become bored with it all and break away. The three Hippies continue their circling movement, no longer linked by hands, but not noticeably bothered by the dispersal of the other "participants" in their ring.

Seven of us arrive at the Avalon at around 11 P.M. The music is already in progress when we get there. There must be at least 300 or more people present. It is one of the most crowded dances I have been to. Many elaborate costumes are worn, attached bells and streamers are flowing from the bodies of some of the people there. There is also the usual smattering of conventionally dressed young people, and, sitting along the side lines, some conventionally dressed older people as well.

The standing, the sitting, and the general milling crowds almost the entire dance floor. It is more concentrated near the stage, in the immediate vicinity of the musicians' stand, but it is not contained there. Many who are not dancing stand around all across the dance floor, and there are clusters of people sitting in the middle of the floor as well. The dancers dance by themselves and "with" others in groups of varying size, in the places between the stationary participants, apparently adjusting their movements to the physical space available for them.

Two or three times during the evening someone starts a serpentining line, which meanders through the stationary participants as well as those dancing, those in the line grabbing out to incorporate both those who are not dancing at the moment and those who are. Some approached join; others do not.

There are two strobe lights at the edge of the dance floor and scattered around the auditorium are some "black lights" as well. Considerable activity seems to be located at these points. People will come one by one, and stand within the area of the blinking strobe lights, moving their bodies in quite similar ways to those who are "dancing" beyond the lights. But the motions under the lights seem to involve much more "looking at one's own body in action" than the dancing. Those moving under the lights will frequently look down at their own feet, out at their own hands before them. Many of those who come under the strobe lights have parts of their body covered with fluorescent paint. These persons seem partially interested in the combination of black lights and the strobe lights, with their painted parts. There is one separate area of black light where those with fluorescent painting on their bodies also wander through. Those just standing and watching often comment when a particularly "effective" outfit walks into the area of the black lights, i.e., when someone in an outfit which is dramatically transformed by the black lights walks through.

I spend most of the time walking around to watch what is going on in various parts of the auditorium. I occasionally encounter the group I have come with, some of them together, some of them with others I have not seen before. Sometimes they nod at me, or smile to me, but none of them ask why I am not dancing. (Such behavior is in sharp contrast to "conventional dances" where I have done the same thing but where I am questioned by my companions about why I am not dancing, but only looking.)

I arrive at the Longshoremen's Hall a few minutes before the first set begins. It is not notably crowded, and those who are there strike me as being generally younger than the usual crowd that can be found at either the Avalon or the Fillmore. There also seem to be many more conventionally dressed participants. However, I would estimate that at least half are "Hippies." Not too many are in "high costume," but rather seem to be wearing their "street clothes" (which is distinctive from conventional dress, but not as elaborate as high costume).

Most of the participants are clustered around the stage where the musicians are playing, but that area is not particularly crowded. Since the hall is very large, the dancers also seem to stay up close to the stage and occasionally they dance in the open areas where those not dancing are sitting and lying around.

On one occasion a solitary dancer stands in the middle of the open area of the dance floor, at quite a distance from the rest of the people, dancing in a very involved manner. A few people along the side lines watch him idly. When I move out to watch from the side lines, a bearded youth comes up to me and asks if I want to dance. I say no, and he goes out on the floor himself. Apparently my participation would have added in some way to his activity, but was in no way necessary to it. However, I have also seen Hippies ask someone to dance, be refused, and ask someone else (though I have no data on the persistence in asking).

A great number of clusters of people seem to be just sitting in the upper balconies in groups of three, four, or more. From there you cannot see the activity on the floor, although you can easily hear the music. The only place where the music is hard to hear is in the lobby, and everyone there seems to be in transition: coming into the auditorium, leaving it, on the way to the bathrooms, going to buy something to drink, or the like.

## THE STRUCTURE OF HIPPIE TIME

Members of the Hippie community of the Haight will frequently say, if asked directly about the matter, that there is "no time" as the conventional society declares it to exist; that the clock and the calendar are cultural conventions superimposed upon the reality of the enormous present that is the world.

Yet in talking between themselves, they will mention having a "good time" or having a "bad time" or remembering "a time when . . ." or thinking about a "time where . . ."

The following field observation provides one such example:

> Lewis starts to talk about getting a job, working, saving up some large sums of money. It sounds as though he is speculating about some real plans, actual actions he intends to undertake. He goes on to say that once he has the money, he will buy a large ship and cruise the Mediterranean. But along the way, without explicitly signifying that he has changed the realm of discourse (any change of voice or facial expression), his description becomes one of fantasy: the ship will go directly from Singapore to San Francisco, it will go under water, and he will stop and see Atlantis.
>
> The three who have been listening to him begin to laugh, responding to the fantasy as fantasy. Lewis says, "None of this is true, you know that. That's why you're laughing."
>
> Iris asks if they treat it as true whether it will be true. He responds, "Yes, for now," and continues to elaborate the fantasy of the ship. By now what he presents as "what will happen" is not presented in the same tone of voice as before, with its speculative quality. Rather, it is presented in the tone of voice and with the inflection one uses when one tells stories to amuse children.
>
> All four become caught up in the adventures, and add parts, elaborating some of Lewis' descriptions. They accept the fact that it is not a true story yet treat the narration seriously.

As a property of the real world for the Hippies of the Haight, "time" is not conceptualized as a quantitative matter of consecutive moments, but a qualitative matter of evaluative significance.[17] The events which constitute the typical Hippie day have no particular community sanctioned *sequence* in which they are to take place. Rather, the decisions members make concerning what practical activity to engage in next are made according to personal preference. Thus, whatever one is doing, regardless of what others may be doing, is characteristically considered to be "where one is at."

However, there are ideologically sanctioned evaluations which can be and frequently are made concerning "where one is at." While the ideology emphasizes an open vista of possibilities for individual action, it also characterizes what ideally should result when each individual freely chooses his course of activity in accordance with the criterion of personal preference. Specifically, (as it is understood by the Hippies of the Haight) living one's life in accordance with their beliefs concerning individual freedom should result in a world that can be characterized by beauty, harmony, psychic satisfaction, and a spiritual community of mankind. In "telling time" in the Haight, (by evaluating experiences) a "good time" is when "where one is at" can be recognized as being in accordance with where one can ideologically expect to be; a "bad time" is where one recognizes a consequential discrepancy between what one ideologically can expect and what one actually encounters.

Similarly, for the Hippies of the Haight, the ideological understanding of "freedom" is a matter of both actual and potential experience. What "is" and what "is not" are treated as elements of psychic consciousness rather than as matters of existential necessity. Thus, the conventional distinction between "past" and "future" as *fixed* times existing before and after the present moment has no ideological justification. However, warrantable judgments of time can be made in terms of psychic consciousness. In telling time in the Haight, "time when . . ." is anything that exists in one's conscious experience; and "time where . . ." anything that can be consciously imagined, even if it has never been experienced.

As a characteristic property of Hippie culture, such a structuring of time as members perceive it appears to be congruent with one of the major axioms of the Hippie ideology: that any given situation, such as "today's life" is to be defined in terms of the simultaneous presence of the physical world and the consciousness of those who exist in the world. Were "time" to march in fixed and serial order, independent of the psychic whim of those who live in that world, this would be a direct violation of the correctness of the ideology itself.[18] Hence, those who think that, as a property of the real world, "time" is defined by consecutive moments which are identical in their duration (like the minutes ticked off by the clock) are, for the Hippies of the Haight, wrong. They do not deny that it is the case that others believe the link between time and the real world is of that nature. But they do assert that others are, if not simply wrong, mistaken, or otherwise uninformed about important matters. And they themselves have strong ideological support for the position they take, as well as the social support of numerous others who also take and sanction that position. Thus, they do not assume that either the clock and the calendar are necessary means for ordering their everyday lives.[19] Rather, for the Hippies of the Haight, time is a structural perspective in an evaluation of events rather than a sequence of events.[20] Once this has been understood, what might otherwise look like aimless, disconnected activity is transformed into a sensible pattern, and one can know "where one is at" although in such a formulation of order, it is irrelevant to ask "where one is going."

## NOTES

1. On the role of "psychic whim," see Chap. 7.
2. In sociable gatherings of Hippies, the display and modeling of various elements of "high costume" by those present occasionally takes

place. The only similar kind of occasion of this type of activity that I am familiar with are sociable gatherings of homosexuals, where someone's collection of "drag" clothing may be brought out during the course of an evening and tried on by everyone present.

3. Leonard Wolf, *Voices of the Love Generation* (Boston: Little, Brown and Co., 1968), p. 176.

4. In this sense, the "open noting" of what the other is preparing to eat would seem to signify the mutual recognition of "members sharing a world in common." A formally similar example is where "protracted" eye contact is used to signify mutual recognition of homosexuals. See Evelyn Hooker, "The Homosexual Community," *Proceedings of the XLV International Congress of Applied Psychology,* Copenhagen, 1961.

5. The general notion, as held by the Hippies, seems to be quite similar to what Melvin Seeman has called the "self-estrangement" meaning of alienation "On the Meaning of Alienation," *American Sociological Review*, Vol. 24 (1959), pp. 789–790.

6. This use of Hip stores is quite analogous to the use of public drinking places as informal gathering places for various collectivities. Cf. Sherri Cavan, *Liquor License* (Chicago: Aldine Publishing Co., 1966), pp. 205–233.

7. Similarly, one of the coffee houses in the District has a sign which is periodically put on the counter, requesting potential customers to be seated and wait until the employees have finished "socializing." The sign goes on to suggest that if the potential customer is in too much of a hurry, perhaps he ought to go elsewhere, since he probably would not fit into the general atmosphere of the establishment anyway.

8. Cf. Fred Davis, "Focus on the Flower Children," *trans*action, Vol. 5 (1967), pp. 10–18.

9. On the basis of the experience of having my mail delivered by Hippie postmen, it sometimes seems that one might not even have to deliver the mail every day. Presumably, the understanding on the part of the Hippies so employed is that if the mail gets to its addressed destination, then the job has "been done," regardless of *when* it gets there.

10. Cf. Chap. 6.

11. "Just Being" is in many respects an unnamed, yet recognizable category of activity, formally similar to those activities Thomas Scheff labels "residual rules." Cf. *Becoming Mentally Ill* (Chicago: Aldine Publishing Co., 1966), pp. 33–39. By and large, it has the general

characteristics of the conventionally designated state of "lolling." Cf. Erving Goffman, *Behavior in Public Places* (London: Collier-Macmillan, 1963).

12. "Being Social" may include smoking grass, watching television, listening to music, going to the movies, walking in the park, going to the museum or the zoo, driving in the country, motorcycling, and a variety of other kinds of activity, either in conjunction with talking, or only occasionally involving talking, or sometimes not involving talking at all.

13. The giving of an indigenous name to a conventional object or event appears to be a way in which the members of a non-conventional group can incorporate the conventional object or event into their way of life, while at the same time they can manage to deny that they and the conventional group have anything in common. In teaching, I have encountered the following kinds of examples: In one of my classes, where I discussed the ethnomethodological perspective in sociology, apparent Hippies have subsequently called it "Psychedelic Sociology." In a deviant behavior class, a militant Black student named his term paper formulation of what I had presented in class as "labeling theory," "Black Sociology." For similar examples, see Gary Schwartz and Don Merton, "The Language of Adolescence," *AJA*, Vol. 72 (1967), pp. 453–468.

14. The specification of "rapping" as such may thus provide a means for members to inform other members of the particular character of the activity, lest others take it for what it was not intended to be. See Edward Hall, "Adumbration as a Feature of Intercultural Communication," *The Ethnography of Communication, American Anthropologist*, Vol. 66, pt. 2 (1964), pp. 154–163.

15. By and large, Hippie communication activity tends to be essentially phatic communication. Cf. Bronislaw Malinowski, in C. K. Ogden and I. A. Richards, *The Meaning of Meaning* (New York: Harcourt Brace and Co., n.d.), supplement I.

16. Given that the Hippie ideology posits that members of the spiritual community will know immediately what the other is talking about, insofar as they share the same consciousness and the same situation, it makes not only good social sense for the members not to request the speaker to exposit on the sense of his assertions, but it also makes good sociological sense. Once an attempt is begun to explicate the meaning of an assertion with exact specification, the likelihood is great that those so engaged will quickly discover that their original understanding may have been quite discrepant all along. Cf. Harold

Garfinkel, *Studies in Ethnomethodology* (Englewood Cliffs, N.J.: Prentice-Hall, 1967), pp. 38–53. This general problem is also noted in W. E. Moore and M. M. Tumin, "Some Social Functions of Ignorance," *ASR*, Vol. 14 (1949), pp. 787–795, in terms of ignorance of viable alternatives serving to reinforce traditional values.

17. The distinction between the Hippie formulation of time and, concurrently, their formulation or order and the conventional American formulation of time and order can be essentially characterized as a distinction between non-lineal and lineal formulations of reality. See Dorothy Lee, "Codifications of Reality: Lineal and Non-Lineal." In *Freedom and Culture* (Englewood Cliffs, N.J.: Prentice-Hall, 1959), pp. 105–120.

18. A rather acute characterization (and commentary) of the ordering of activity in conventional life is contained in the Beatles', "A Day in the Life," in the Sgt. Pepper album.

19. Such sequencing of activity provides at least a partial solution to the problem of social organization by coordinating members' activity over time. The problem of social organization may also be (again, at least partially) solved by coordinating members' activity in space. Similarly, both temporal and ecological ordering may be employed, with correspondingly greater uniformity of action. Cf. Sherri Cavan, *Liquor License* (Chicago: Aldine Publishing Co., 1966), pp. 88–111, Erving Goffman, *Asylums* (Garden City, N.Y.: Doubleday Anchor, 1961), pp. 1–125, and William Rosengren and Spencer DeVault, "The Sociology of Time and Space in an Obstetrical Hospital," in E. Friedson, ed., *The Hospital in Modern Society* (London: Collier-Macmillan, 1963), pp. 266–292. For a more general discussion, see: O. L. S. Shackle, *Decision, Order and Time* (Cambridge: Cambridge University Press, 1961), Wilbert Moore, *Man, Time and Society* (New York: John Wiley and Sons, 1963), and Amos Hawley, *Human Ecology* (New York: The Ronald Press, 1950).

20. In effect, telling time in the Haight is much like telling time in Nuerland: it is calculated in terms of relationships between events. Cf. Evans-Pritchard, "Nuer Time Reckoning," *Africa*, Vol. 12 (1939), p. 208. A similar formulation of time in American society is found in ghetto street life. See John Horton, "Time and Cool People," *trans-action*, IV (1967) pp. 5–12.

# 6

# How To Obtain Grass
# in the Haight

For the Hippies of the Haight, to ask "where one is at" is to ask
for an evaluation of how one is doing in life. In answer to such
questions, members of the Hippie community do not describe
themselves as "early" or "late," "ahead" or "behind." [1] They do
not conceptualize life as a progression of activities that can then
serve as a standard to evaluate whether they are "in time." Rather,
they conceptualize life as a matter of varying experiences that are
to be judged by their particular nature. In answer to the question
of how they are doing in life, members respond that they are
"grooving" or "hassling," "tripping out" or "on a bummer." Such
descriptions constitute interpretations of the social meaning of
actual states of affairs. They are the sanctioned ways by which
members refer to their experiences.

The actual state of their circumstances may be reviewed at
any time by the members of any group. When one asks "where
one is at" (or, in conventional terms, "where one is going") one
calls for an accounting of how the present situation measures up
to general standards of how the world-should-be-in-general within
the ideological perspective of the Hippies. In the Haight, a

member knows, in the most general sense, when to answer "groovy" and when to answer "hassling," when to answer "tripping out" and when to answer "on a bummer." He constructs an answer from his practical evaluation of the nature of his present situation. Not "everything" is a "Hippie thing," nor is "every Hippie thing" a "groovy Hippie thing." For example, obtaning drugs is a routine Hippie thing. But for the members of the community, it may not always be a "groovy" thing; more often than not it's a "hassle." And sometimes it's a "bummer."

In the present chapter, I shall focus on the relationship of the ideological beliefs held by the Hippies of the Haight and those evaluative judgments they make concerning their experiences in "obtaining drugs." For purposes of analysis, I shall focus only on the nature and evaluation of marijuana transactions, for these tend to be the most prevalent and the most visible drug transactions in the community.[2]

## RELEVANT IDEOLOGICAL CONSIDERATIONS

The belief system of a group generates a symbolic superstructure that hovers over the members' practical day-to-day existence. It provides that day-to-day existence with its justification, as well as the scheme whereby daily life is to be made sensible. Once established, this belief (or ethical) system also influences the actual nature of members' collective practices. It sets the terms by which the definition of the situation becomes reality—reifications that further activities must address if the members are to anticipate a successful and sensible outcome from such activities.[3] In this sense, if a particular complex of ethics and values did not exist in the Haight Hippie community, "obtaining grass" as a practical activity might occur quite differently from the way it was observed.[4] For example, it might occur as a straight underworld economic enterprise, governed only by the economic laws of supply and demand. Accounts of such organization of drug transactions can be found with respect to the large-scale illegal drug enterprise.[5] But drug transactions among self-identified members of the Hippie community do not look like the drug transactions in organized crime, nor like the general economic transactions of the conventional marketplace in American society. A sociological accounting for this difference takes into consideration the conditions set by the elements of ethics and values that enter into the members' understanding of what the Hippie community is and what "obtaining grass" means within that system.

The ideology of spiritual community proclaims that the essence of life is to be found in the love of and for one's fellow man. The existence of such love is to be demonstrated in behavioral terms by ethical maxims such as the following: "Consider the interests of your fellow man as well as your own interests." "Do not use your fellow man for instrumental purposes, as a means of satisfying your own personal purposes." "Share and give what there is available; treat what is available as though it belonged to the community of man in general."

Beliefs about hallucinogenic drugs in the Hippie community have two sanctioned interpretations. In both interpretations, drugs are important for "expanding" one's consciousness; they create a situation where one not only becomes aware of his psyche as a part of himself, but aware of the potential of that psyche. The interpretations differ essentially in whether 1) drugs are believed to be necessary and sufficient for this expansion of the consciousness; or 2) they are believed to be a tool to affect it.[6]

In the first interpretation, the hallucinogenic effects of drugs (particularly LSD, but also peyote, psilocybin, mescaline, marijuana, STP, DMT) are the direct and essentially only cause of the initial vision.

Statements such as these from *Voices of the Love Generation* are illustrative of this interpretation:

"LSD puts you in touch with your surroundings. You take LSD and your surroundings are there. Feelings about your surroundings are there. The onion is peeled and peeled and peeled, and in the center we have something that is really an incredible thing. It's where we're able to see from more accurately, and more honestly, and without a great deal of incredible amounts of effort . . . (the use of these drugs) automatically puts people in a different frame of reference. It points out a lot of inequities in the system. Just by their existence; by the fact that they are suppressed." [7]

"I went to a psychiatrist when I was twenty-three . . . I took some LSD. I took quite a lot of it before I went to the psychiatrist, but one time I took it when I went down the coast and I ended up running naked on the highway and really flipped out. My mother had to come down and take me. . . . My mother said 'You have to go to a psychiatrist' . . .
"What about the acid trip? Wasn't that supposed to help?"
"Yeah, it did. I could never have gotten where I am now without the acid." [8]

Within the framework of this interpretation, anyone who has not fully accepted the drug experience cannot fully understand and acknowledge the truth of the ideology; for the vision upon which it is built is missing.

Furthermore, anyone who utilizes drugs is destined to see the vision in its ideologically postulated form. "Freaking-out" and to a lesser extent "bad trips" are thus explained in terms of the user being in a bad situation: either not prepared to understand the meaning of the vision; too caught up in the conventional world to accept the implications of the vision, even if he understands them; or surrounded by incongruent elements, so that there is no opportunity for the drugs to "properly" affect him.

The first example below comes from *Voices of the Love Generation*; the second from field observations:

"I've had psilocybin, mescaline, peyote, and datura and methedrine. I'm going to take STP. I'm kind of afraid of it but I'm going to take it . . . I feel my fear is that there'll be a revelation of something that I'm not yet willing to accept the consequences of. I feel I must if it's the truth. So I'm going to take it." [9]

Carol is telling Nora and me about the "bad trip" her roommate had recently experienced. Carol explains that some friend of Ann, her roommate, brought Ann home "high and screaming." The evening was spent with the roommate sitting naked on the bed. Carol goes on to say, "She screamed all night—terrible cries. I thought she would never stop."

Nora asks if it was the roommate's first trip and Carol replies, "No. I don't know how many times she's dropped acid before. But it's a lot."

I ask why this was such a bad trip for her and Carol answers, "It was the situation she was in," although she cannot explain what the situation was like, other than to say, "It was a bad scene. She shouldn't have dropped it [taken acid] there."

In the second interpretation, drugs are not central but only a means or a tool to assist the user in breaking the bonds of the perspective of the world, and the accompanying ideology, that he has accepted all his life. But the drugs do not themselves transform persons.

> "What makes you reach for a drug and what's in it for you? You personally."
> "It's always different. Sometimes maybe to disguise feelings. Sometimes to blow them up, sometimes maybe not to think. A lot of reasons, a lot of different drugs."
> "Is there no moral imperative in acid?"
> "I don't think so. Look at acid dealers. Acid dealers carry guns around. They take it. They've had it." [10]

The following excerpt from the introduction to a guide for "successful" drug experience sums up this interpretation:

> "ACID—LSD: Although acid has no value in and of itself—will not make you holy or good or wise or anything else except high—it can be used in a valuable way. It can be an educational tool; you can learn something from it." [11]

For those employing this interpretation, there are means other than drugs which can be used to attain the vision: meditation, Eastern religions, and, to some extent, Western religion.

Therefore, as the hallucinogenic drugs are only a tool of bringing about the vision, they may be put to other uses as well.

One of the community members notes in *Voices of the Love Generation*:

> "I think drugs are being used for everything . . . I think I see drugs being used . . . to open up the sexual synapse in the head and to get some of that conditioning out of the way. Acid is a great deconditioning agent . . . I think that perhaps drugs are being used for every possible reason . . . the same reasons that cars are used. Some people fuck in their cars. Some people use their cars to take them to and from work. Some people just go for a ride in their cars, to be alone. Some people take a car only to use once in a while. It's a tool." [12]

Within this second interpretation of the role of drugs, what the user will "find" during the course of his use is not guaranteed. He may find the vision which is at the basis of the ideology, but he may also encounter visions which are in no way compatible with that ideology.[13]

> We have been sharing a table in the cafe with some members of the Hell's Angels, chatting idly about what their "scene" is like. At one point, one of them begins to recount what he describes as "one of the best experiences I've ever had." The nature of the experience was essentially a rumble between himself and some other Angels and some Black males. At the conclusion of the account, he says, "Those Hippies say that if you fight or something like that on acid you'll freak out. They don't know what they're talking about. It was the best fight I was ever in, that fight when I was on acid. Beautiful. Just beautiful."

Regardless of which particular interpretation of the drug experience a member uses, the Hippies of the Haight generally acknowledge the relationship of drug use to the recognition and implementation of the ideological tenets which originally justify the community. Drug use as a course of action on the part of the members is comprehensible, perceived as legitimate, and frequently undertaken.[14] Within the Hippie community, then, the smoking of marijuana is a regular and recurrent activity for "good reasons" which members can and will provide.

## THE PROBLEM OF SUPPLY

Drug use as a general course of action subsumes a number of separate events within the Hippie community. As Becker has noted, becoming a user includes having available a framework for interpreting the experience. "(1) learning to smoke the drug in a way which will produce real effects; (2) learning to recognize the effects and connect them with drug use (learning, in other words, to get high); and (3) learning to enjoy the sensations. . ." [15]

However, Becker goes on to say,

> Learning to enjoy marijuana is a necessary but not sufficient condition for a person to develop a stable pattern of drug use. He has still to contend with forces of social control that make the act seem inexpedient, immoral, or both. [16]

The illegal status of marijuana in the encompassing society means that even where an individual possesses the framework for interpreting the experience, actual use of the drug as a regular and recurrent course of action will be dependent upon solving the problems of supply, secrecy, and morality as they are posed by the conventional society.

Let us consider "smoking grass" as a general course of action subsuming four separate events: having an interpretive framework, having a congruent morality, having an available supply, and having conditions of secrecy. [17] It should be obvious that these separate elements have variable characters. Two of them (having an interpretive framework and having a congruent morality) are, once achieved, no longer problematic. [18] Once they have been learned, they merge into the area of subsidiary awareness in the ongoing course of "smoking grass."

The other two (supply and secrecy) are eminently practical matters: the members' theoretical knowledge of how supply and secrecy are to be managed is always a matter of focal awareness for them. [19] These matters have day-to-day implications each time "smoking grass" comes up as a prospective course of action. They are in effect recurrent practical problems to be solved regularly by the members of the Hippie community. For the purpose of the present analysis, I shall address only one of them—that of supply; for this is the most problematic issue.

Drug transactions take place in a variety of ways. In one set of situations they are simply economic transactions, as where two people with no interest in the actual use of the drugs are involved in importing and distributing. In another situation we find the "professional deal," where a wholesaler makes a transaction with a street dealer, who in turn sells directly to users. The street dealer may also have an interest in the drug for his own use; but this is only one interest he has. His transaction with the wholesaler is still a straightforward exchange, governed essentially by economic principles and the general limitations imposed by exchange of illegal commodities (i.e., the transaction cannot be carried out openly).

Marijuana also moves from the street dealer to the street buyer (whose only intended purpose with the drugs is use). But by the time it moves into the streets of the Hippie community, "obtaining grass" is no longer like "obtaining any commodity whatsoever." Now marijuana transactions become an eminently cultural event. The procedure for this event is not an arbitrary matter; it is generally treated as something special which must be understood by the participants if it is to be concluded successfully. When marijuana moves from the street dealer to the street buyer, "how to obtain grass in the Haight" is formally the same as "how to ask for a drink in Subanum."

As Frake writes,[20]

> Ward Goodenough has proposed that a description of a culture—an ethnography—should properly specify what it is that a stranger to a society would have to know in order to appropriately perform any role in any scene staged by the society. If an ethnographer of Subanum were to take this notion seriously, one of the most crucial sets of instructions to provide would be that specifying how to ask for a drink. Anyone who cannot perform this operation successfully will be automatically excluded from

the stage upon which some of the most dramatic scenes of Subanum life are performed.

## OBTAINING GRASS

"Obtaining grass" rests on a basic formal procedure: a transaction between one who desires and one who has grass such that, at the end of the transaction, the one who wants it now "has grass," and can tell whether or not his transaction was successful. Criteria the participants will consider in this evaluation are (1) the unit of transaction (or amount involved in it); (2) the mode whereby the transaction is undertaken; and (3) the quality of the transaction. These three factors are the components for essentially "knowing what you are doing when you obtain grass in the Haight" for the participants. These factors are variably interrelated, however. For example, the sanctioned unit is not fixed, but dependent upon the mode of transaction. The sanctioned unit when the transactional mode is that of a gift is not the same as that for a purchase. Whether one has obtained the grass in a "good deal" or not is variably dependent not only upon the transaction unit and mode, but the quality of the merchandise as well. Obtaining grass can be evaluated by the participants with a focus upon one factor or another (depending on purposes for entering the transaction). For purposes of explication here, we will focus on the mode of transaction as the independent variable and the unit and evaluation of the transaction as dependent variables. This scheme produces four recognizable practices for obtaining grass in the Haight: buying grass, "laying grass," giving grass, and requesting grass.

### *1. Buying Grass*

At some point or other, virtually all the marijuana supply available in the Haight comes into the community from members engaged in "buying grass." Both the legal and the meteorological climate of the area preclude any systematic cultivation of the plant. In effect, regardless of their ideological tenets, the members of the Haight are not a self-contained community, and the community ideology must be modified by the practical issue of treating grass as a commodity in an economic transaction. Such modifications emerge on an ad hoc basis reflecting economic and legal contingencies. How one "buys" grass in the Haight is not thus treated as entirely independent of the ideological system. However, these economic and legal contingencies are managed *in terms of* the ideological system.

"Buying grass" as a mode of transaction takes place whenever a user exchanges conventional money for the marijuana that he will eventually use. In this transaction, the factors of unit and evaluation are all entwined with the mode of transaction; for unlike the other modes by which one can obtain grass, buying introduces as an integral part of the transaction the ideologically irrelevant but practically necessary factor of money. How one buys in terms of what amount of money one pays is decided in terms of two criteria: the unit of transaction and the quality expected of it.

The main problems involved in "buying grass" in the Haight can be illustrated by the problems faced by the street dealer (i.e., any seller, regardless of the extent of his activity.) [21] As those involved in selling have said at various times: "The biggest problem for a dealer is to sell it at a profit without looking like there is a profit."

That is, given the ideological tenet of spiritual community, selling for anything more than what one paid initially is behavior contrary to the ethical precepts of the community. The dealers attempt to manage the discrepancy between their actions and the ideology by keeping their actual buying price a closely guarded secret and then justifying their selling price in terms of general-market-conditions-that-are-beyond-our-control. The dealers' "explanation" for the price of marijuana is virtually always phrased in such terms. If the street dealers are successful in keeping their wholesale price secret, the end result is that those who buy their grass from even known and reputable dealers on the street have no firm idea of the wholesale price. But usually the street buyers are somewhat skeptical about what they are told of the wholesale price from sellers. Apparently, the idea that the dealers *may* be making a profit while paying lip service to the community ideology comes as no surprise to the buyers. Yet, demand for the commodity forces sellers to accept the dealer's word—or go without. Hence, in talking about grass during the period of these observations, street buyers would quote the going price of a "key" (a kilogram of average quality) as anywhere from 80 to 150 dollars. Furthermore, the going price of a key is a regular and recurrent topic of conversation among users, as they attempt collectively to discern what the present price of a key "really" is, i.e., what the wholesale market price is, independent of what any particular street dealer may tell them.[22]

The following field incident is indicative of the general problem involved in the street buyers' evaluation of their transactions:

> In the course of conversation about other matters, Tony mentions to Mark and myself that he can "get a key of Acapulco Gold for $250." He then goes on to say, "It's real gold, I've had some" but he wants to know if $250 is a good price.
>
> Tony is not entirely naïve. He has been in the drug scene for as long as I have known him (close to five years). I don't remember any other time transactions have come up in conversation with him, other than his occasionally mentioning that Ed has some methedrine or some cocaine, or someone "just got" some new (presumably ordinary) grass. I have no idea what his regular sources are.
>
> However, Tony's present problem is that, given that he is sure that what he will get for his money is "real Gold," he is at the same time not sure how much money he should put out for it— what would be a "fair price," where what he took in for his money would be equivalent in value to the money he put out.
>
> Mark responds to Tony's problem by saying that he doesn't know the price for a key of "real Gold," at least "not around here" (implying that he knows it for other places but that won't be much help). He tells Tony that he will try to find out.
>
> A few days later, Mark tells me to tell Tony that he has been talking to some people in the area and they think the maximum

equitable price for a key of "real Gold" would be $200: that Tony would be getting a "bad deal" if he paid $250 for it.

The problem of how the buyers come to terms with estimating the wholesale price of a kilo may also be affected by their understanding of the conditions of supply. Thus in 1967, when two border guards were shot at Tijuana, rumors quickly circulated in the general community about the effect the incident would have on the available source, and what this in turn would do to the price of kilos. While it was never clearly established that the incident was relevant to the illegal importation of marijuana to the United States, two dealers I knew at that time were quite quick to raise the price of their stock on hand and to explain that price in terms of the "scarcity because of what happened at Tijuana." It is possible that others may have done the same.[23]

Similarly, conversations among street dealers typically have the character of the obverse of conversations among street buyers. Where buyers in collective encounters attempt to estimate the "actual" wholesale price, the dealers in collective encounters attempt to estimate what the retail market "will stand."

The buyers' general uncertainty of the wholesale price of average quality grass is even more acute in terms of "quality" grass—any grass known or thought to produce a particularly "fine high." Hence, when street dealers manage to buy a key of "Gold,"[24] what they can sell it for on the street is uncertain. The following excerpts from field notes provide one example of this uncertainty:

> Walt has just purchased Gold, which he announces is "very good stuff": it is resinous and clean (i.e., has relatively few sticks and twigs in it). Rick, another dealer present, agrees to Walt's estimation of the quality—on the basis of appearance and sampling.
> Walt says he has purchased the key for $300 and he is planning to sell it for $15 an ounce (approximately $5 more than the going price for average quality grass). Rick remarks that that is not enough. It is very good grass and Walt can make more on it.

Walt agrees and more or less decides to sell it for $20 an ounce ("more or less" because while he is sitting on the floor abstractly cleaning it he is also muttering about the idea of possibly getting $25 an ounce for it).

Walt and Rick continue to debate the possible price for almost an hour. Eventually Rick asks Walt, "If you re going to sell it, why are you cleaning it? It will weigh more if you don't clean it" (i.e., sell it with seeds and stems).

Rick's remark is taken by Walt as an indication that he could probably easily get $25 a cleaned ounce for it. The matter has still not been finally settled when I leave, although the next day I found out that, at least to his "close" friends, he was selling it for $20 a cleaned ounce. (The mention of the price to his "close" friends seemed to imply that there might be another price for "mere" friends.) [25]

The street dealers' collective estimates of what the street market of the community will stand and the subsequent action they take upon those estimates derive from careful consideration of what they anticipate as the situation of the street buyers. This consideration is weighed in terms of the sellers' understanding of the buyer's ideological allegiance. To be a street dealer, then, one must be able to take a particular kind of perspective toward the ideological structure of the community, one from which the possibility of manipulating the ideology to one's individual advantage can be seen.[26]

The variant perspective of the street buyer and the street dealer can be seen in the following two field examples. The first took place at a gathering where none of those present had experience in dealing or wholesale buying; the second took place in a setting composed entirely of occasional and systematic street dealers.

Leonard and Stan are talking about the price of grass in the area. Leonard mentions that the street dealers "make a healthy profit" from their transactions. Leonard's voice carries a measure of disgust, and Stan responds in kind, contemplating the kind of "moral character" one would have to have to live off "that kind of money." By the end of the discussion, both have expressed somewhat heated annoyance with "street dealers in general" although Stan concludes the discussion by saying that "his dealer" is not like that.

There are three dealers present, talking idly about business in general. I mention the amount of profit being made on the street in marijuana transactions and both Tom and Alex acknowledge the implied discrepancy between the community ideology of sharing, reciprocity, mutuality, and the actual individualistic behavior that takes place. However, their acknowledgment has the sound and character of a comment on some distant activity, as though they were casually commenting on some group in Kansas, a group they hardly knew, have little interest in, and no involvement with. To my remark, Tom says "yeah," in a very flat tone, and Alex remarks, "That's the way it is there," in a kind of philosophically-realistic way. The other dealer simply ignored my remark altogether.

On numerous observed occasions the buyers' understanding of what the dealers may be up to formed an integral issue in their conversation on "how to buy grass." The most preferable way to buy grass is to "know your dealer." This does not necessarily require prolonged experiences of marijuana transactions with him. "Know" in this context means to have knowledge of him outside the contact of marijuana transactions: to be linked into a friendship network with him, or at least linked with someone who knows him in this way.

The legions of "unknown" street dealers who can be found in the area are thus to be considered only as "last resort sources." Exchanges can be expected to result in "poor" transactions, either because the commodity is likely to be overpriced, or of very poor quality, or both. In effect, to know how properly to obtain grass in the Haight is dependent in part on first knowing how to make friends in the Haight.

Most users "buy grass" in the Haight by the "lid": customarily, a small plastic bag containing about 1½ ounces of loose, uncleaned grass, wrapped in a thick roll shape and sealed with either Scotch or masking tape.[27] Unless there is something notable about the quality of the high produced from it, a "good lid" is a transaction unit which involves grass of the proper weight, without too many sticks and twigs. (Sticks and twigs add to the weight of the unit, but have no effect if used).

Occasionally, buying grass takes place in units smaller than a lid, although I have only heard about such transactions in conversations of general users and not seen any of them. They say, at least in the Haight, that the most usual unit less a lid in size is a "box": a small matchbox containing well-cleaned grass (no seeds or sticks) and weighing about half an ounce.

However, in buying grass in the Haight, a box is acceptable only if you cannot afford a more expensive lid. In the same way, pre-rolled joints are undesirable units among regular users. Although they are available and sold in the area, it is generally understood among the members of the Hippie community that "they are sold to 'tourists' (and other non-members) who don't know what they are doing in the first place."

Such a judgment about the purchasers of pre-rolled joints is based on the members' general understanding and knowledge of marijuana transactions as they take place between street dealers and street buyers, as well as the variant attitudes of members about "how to smoke grass." Accounts given by members as to why they do not buy pre-rolled joints, and why one should not, include the following kinds of assertions:

1. The final quantity you end up with is dubious. You can't go by the weight of the joints alone, because they are usually rolled up "fat" (at least the circumference of a regular cigarette) and hence the amount of marijuana in the joint may be padded out with non-drug substances, such as oregano. It is possible for the same kind of padding to take place in a lid and there are stories of it taking place, but it is even more "certain" that it might happen with a "box" than it is with a "lid."

Victims of such "unfair" transactions are not likely to be regular users, however, since what you have to know to be a regular user includes within it what you have to know to evaluate whether you have, or will get, a fair transaction.[28] Specifically, while strained oregano "looks like grass," if one cleans one's own grass, one can tell by the composition of the lid whether oregano has been added. If oregano has been added, there will be a "disproportionate" amount of loose, fine leaves.

2. Among regular users, there is a variable belief about the optimum size of a joint. Some believe in "fat" or "moderately fat" joints as minimally adequate for the aim of two or more people getting high. Others believe in a "thin" or very thin joint (a "matchstick joint") as superior. The latter group usually argues that irrespective of the actual amount of marijuana the joint contains, a thin joint takes in more air when you "toke" (drag) on it than "fat" joints. Thus, for the latter group, pre-rolled joints, which tend to be fat, are a waste of good grass.

3. Finally, there is a variable lore of the most satisfactory and aesthetic way of smoking marijuana, which includes stylistic preferences for kinds of paper (regular white, straw, or commercially flavored papers) in cigarette form or in a pipe. Pre-rolled joints do not allow for any stylistic flexibility.

Thus, when buying grass, one can anticipate that one will have "done well in the transaction" if one buys lids of uncleaned grass from street dealers who are either known directly or indirectly to the buyer outside of the transaction situation. However, while one can anticipate success of the endeavor under these conditions, one cannot assert the certainty of the outcome in advance. These criteria merely provide the necessary features for a transaction of "good prospects."

How one knows what he finally got—how one is eventually and properly to evaluate the purchase—is to be understood in terms of the "quality" of what was bought. For example, "unfair activities" by wholesalers may result in impaired average grass. At least in the Haight, one of the constant issues of conversation for both street buyers and street dealers considering the purchase of a key is whether the marijuana has been "cured in sugar"—a process which results in increasing the weight but not the "high." It is "unfair activity" because quality is understood in terms of the extent of the high in relationship to the amount of marijuana smoked in order to produce it. Not only does sugar-cured grass give less high (which some non-sugar-cured grass may do as well), but it is understood that "from smoking it you can develop a very sore throat and a bad (harsh) cough." One of the normal vicissitudes of obtaining grass in the Haight is its variable quality; and so this is one kind of normal trouble the buyer can encounter in buying. Hence, as long as one gets a full measure that is reasonably clean, one is expected to evaluate the transaction as a "good one" even though it involved poor-quality marijuana. On the other hand, if one gets a cough or a sore throat, one now has good reason for saying he "got burned."

## 2. *Laying Grass*

"Laying grass" is the only mode of transaction for which there is a special linguistic phrase in the Haight, presumably because "laying grass" is the mode of transaction which most fully embodies the ideology of spiritual community. The members of the Hippie community speak of "someone laying grass on someone else" when the mode of transaction is to give the grass to another as an unsolicited gift. In such cases of transactions, the unit is usually "about half an ounce" [29] of finely cleaned grass. The containers observed in this mode of transaction have been small metal film cans, typewriter ribbon cans, small tobacco cans, or plastic Baggies. The amount of grass almost entirely fills the container in which it is given only in the metal film containers (although it comes close in the smaller sized typewriter ribbon cans). However, in spite of the variable sizes of the containers in which grass is "laid on" another, the amount customarily appears to be "half an ounce."

Any transaction by which one has obtained grass by having it "laid on" him is spoken of as a "good" transaction. Since "laying grass" involves by definition a substantial unit, the actual quality of the grass need not be taken into consideration with respect to the evaluation of the transaction. That is, poor quality grass is to be simply treated as "grass" and the transaction is always a "good" one, although superior quality grass usually serves to define the transaction as an "extraordinarily good one."

"Giving grass" to someone is distinguished from "laying grass on someone" by the size of the unit involved. In neither instance (giving or laying) does the recipient instigate the transaction. However, one speaks of having "laid some grass on someone" or "having had some laid on oneself" only when the unit involved constitutes loose, clean grass in at least an amount of "half an ounce."

## 3. Giving Grass

"Giving grass" is spoken of casually as just that. Ideologically, it constitutes "the least someone can do." But one has not been given grass if all that has been transacted is a "toke." That is, to enter a place where a joint is being smoked and to be offered it for your smoking does not constitute "having been given grass." [30] Situations where one is invited to share a joint are effectively below the level of awareness of the members of the community, something done automatically, as when members of the conventional community nod to an acquaintance, but do not say anything.

In the Haight, one has been "given grass" when one has been presented with the gift of one or more joints, separate and distinct from the smoking of any particular joint. (One may be given grass and then immediately offer to smoke the joint so given with the giver. But this still constitutes having been "given grass," since the offer to share a joint obtained in this way is not required.)

The giving of one joint by one member to another may be made with no particular comment on the part of the giver. Or it may be prefaced with a remark such as "I thought you would like /appreciate this." Such remarks usually preface that which is to be considered particularly good quality grass.

In general, then, one "gives grass" in the Haight by presenting to the other one or more pre-rolled joints as an event separate and distinct from simply "smoking grass" together.

### 4. Requesting Grass

Occasionally, requests are made by acquaintances for grass in situations where one person has some grass which is being smoked there and then. "Requesting grass" is thus yet another mode of obtaining grass, although during the course of my observations it was infrequent. And the only situations in which I have observed it are situations where "smoking grass" has been taking place and the smoking occasion is ending. The grass which is involved in the transaction is characteristically clean and always loose, since such smoking occasions ordinarily do not involve pre-rolled joints.

Customarily, one "requests grass" in the Haight by saying to the one possessing the grass-in-use, "Can I get some grass from you?" The requester typically implies by tone of voice that he will pay for it, and he may make that intent explicit. However, payment in these situations seems to have the character of a polite fiction: when the offer for payment has been made, I have never seen it accepted by the owner. It would seem that it is mutually understood that while it is proper for the requester to offer to pay, it would be an impropriety for the other to accept.[31]

The ideology sanctions as acceptable both the request and the compliance with it. But "requesting grass" is the most problematic means of "obtaining grass." If the moral maxim of sharing were accepted in the strict letter of the formulation, obtaining grass by requesting it from anyone who has it leaves open the possibility of ideologically sanctioned exploitation within the group: "Ask and ye shall be given," anytime and anyplace.

As a means of avoiding exploitive extremes, it is understood that while, ideologically, one "can" request grass anytime there is some available to be requested, regularly and routinely obtaining your supply this way is negatively viewed and also is likely to lead to a reevaluation of one's status of "member-in-good-standing." However, the situation must still be managed by the *one from whom* the request is made. Unless the one requesting already has a "reputation" for extensive requests, the one from whom the request is made is ethically obligated to comply, regardless of his personal preferences in the matter. Thus, obtaining grass by "requesting," is an event quite distinct from receiving it unsolicited.

I have never seen the giver, for example, roll one or more joints from the supply available and present these to the requester. Rather, "giving on request" (in contrast to "just giving") involves clean, loose grass—the supply in use. If the giver has a visible substantial supply (e.g., clearly more than an ounce), he will put into a Baggie (or some other suitable container) what "looks" equivalent to half an ounce: what "looks" equivalent to the unsolicited gift that is "laid on." But on most observed occasions the actual amount seems to have been somewhat less—perhaps between ⅓ and 2/5 of an ounce. However, because nothing is weighed out in the transaction, but rather only visually estimated in terms of what is put into the bag, neither the receiver (nor the observer, in this case) can say for sure what has been given there and then. It can in effect "look" like "half an ounce" or it can look like "less than half an ounce," depending on what one thinks it will be.[32]

On the other hand, if the donor's supply is not visibly substantial (e.g., if it only looks as if there is an ounce or so there) it is "divided," although here there is no attempt to make it look like an equitable (50-50) division. More customarily it is openly divided into approximately ⅓ for the requester and ⅔ for the donor.

What seems to be involved in the giving of units of requested grass is the understanding of the practical application of the moral maxim of sharing. The possessor's observable supply is taken to bear a direct relation to what he ultimately "has"—either in terms of an actual "stash," general accessibility, financial availability, or in terms of all three. If the possessor has "a lot" on hand (i.e., clearly *more* than a cleaned ounce; at least two or three ounces or more) then he is presumed to be in the position to "lay it on" the other—voluntarily to share what he has. And thus it means to give unsolicited at least half an ounce. To "lay grass" on the other is an ideologically valued activity—it is something a "good" Hippie would do. Hence, when the possessor is solicited and he has a substantial supply, an attempt is made to make it look as if the grass is really being "laid on" the requester—that the requester is getting a full half an ounce. Members expect that such an interchange should take place if it is possible for the possessor to do it, since it is ideologically right that he do it if he can. While "laying grass" is the ideological ideal, independent of persons and personal preference, in observation of actual practice it is not frequent, as the following field excerpts indicate.

> Peter brings out some grass and mentions, in passing, that "someone laid it on me the other day." Both Carla and Warren seem quite surprised, as though such an event were not a usual one.

> Beth is talking about a friend of hers who has been living in the country. She says her friend has "laid" some grass on her twice in the past three months. One of the girls in the group asks, "Does he grow his own?" and Beth answers no. The matter is dropped at this point, but the apparent implication of the girl's question was that such activity on the part of Beth's friend must be due to some extraordinary circumstances such as having a large amount of grass freely available.

In contrast, where the possessor's supply is not both apparently and clearly substantial, no attempt need be made to give the impression of an equitable division because there is no ideological necessity for it. The ideological tenets of the community do not stress self-abnegation for the benefit of the other, but rather mutual sharing as an equitable matter whenever possible. The possessor's visibly smaller supply is taken as indicating at least a smaller possible supply for now. Therefore, one need comply with the moral maxim of sharing only as it is possible to do so without any particular cost to oneself. In effect, then, by giving only ⅓ of what is visibly there, one can still be a "good" member, since it is "open and apparent" (it is a matter that anyone can see) that this is the best the donor can possibly do at the present, without completely ignoring his own interests.

## EVALUATIONS AS IDEOLOGICAL INTERPRETATIONS

If the ideological value of a spiritual community of mankind —and its concomitant moral maxim of sharing—were the only issue for the Hippies of the Haight to consider, one would not expect them to sanction obtaining "grass" by buying it. However, sharing is apparently not the only relevant ideological issue for members to consider in evaluating "how to obtain grass."

It is in "buying grass" that the ideological meaning of monetary transactions becomes specifically relevant. While money is generally defined as possessing no ideological meaning in and of itself, it is recognized as a negotiable token of exchange until further notice: specifically, until "the rest of the city is liberated." Hence, in monetary transactions, what specifically becomes relevant for the Hippies of the Haight is an evaluation of the "fairness" of the exchange. The criteria for the assessment of the fairness of the exchange are the cost, (in terms of monies expended) in relation to the quality of the merchandise received (in terms of the perceived adequacy of the "high" produced).

However, matters such as cost and quality, which are employed as criteria for judging monetary transaction, are not relevant for judging social transactions. In social transactions, as when "laying grass," what is relevant is that the amount involved in any particular transaction look like "the proper amount" as compared to "the proper amount" for "giving grass."

Perhaps the ambiguous position which "requesting grass" seems to have rests on an ideological paradox: on the basis of the ideological tenets, any member can ask anything of other members of the spiritual community while at the same time, no member should have his particular course of action obstructed—which would be the obverse of "do your own thing." In effect, while the sanctioned practice is "to ask," "having to give" is censured. Perhaps, then, requesting grass is ordinarily not assessed, lest the ideologically problematic status of the practice be made explicit.

Furthermore, as noted in the following chapter, the smoking of marijuana is considered an important aspect of the general maintenance of members' psyches. Thus, for those who intend to obtain drugs, there is high value accorded to carrying out successful transactions. At the same time, there is risk associated with the endeavors of those who have drugs which can be obtained by others. As a practical condition of the community life, grass must be imported into the District. As the members understand their world, not only is being "busted" (arrested) worse when one is dealing—in contrast to merely possessing—but busts of dealers are considered a more likely event than busts for mere possession. Thus, the evaluations of the various kinds of drug transactions invoke not only relevant ideological tenets which members hold, but also members' practical understanding of the meaning of "trouble." However, as I shall suggest in the following chapter, a member's sanctioned recognition of "trouble" is itself a matter which is formulated within the ideological framework of the community.

## NOTES

1. Cf. Julius Roth, *Timetables* (Indianapolis, Ind.: The Bobbs-Merrill Co., 1963), p. 94.

2. The data I have available on transactions involving other valued drugs in the community (acid, speed, DMT, and a few others) suggest that, in their general form, transactions involving these drugs are quite similar to transactions involving marijuana. There are differences as well, but for the present purposes, they will not concern us here.

3. Friedrich Engels makes this point quite explicit when he states

that once the bourgeois mentality has conceived of the law, the law must be just unto itself, even if this subsequently affects the vested interest of the bourgeois adversely. Karl Marx and Friedrich Engels, *Basic Writings on Politics and Philosophy*, L. S. Feuer, ed. (Garden City, N.Y.: Doubleday Anchor, 1959), p. 404. For a more general discussion see Peter Berger and Thomas Luckman, *The Social Construction of Reality* (Garden City, N.Y.: Doubleday and Co., 1966), pp. 45–118, and Karl Mannheim, *Ideology and Utopia* (New York: Harcourt, Brace and Co., n.d.), pp. 98–108.

4. This issue of how the belief system of a group effects the particular course of action selected by members from the possible alternatives available was one of the major problems addressed by Max Weber in *The Protestant Ethic and the Spirit of Capitalism* (New York: Charles Scribner's Sons, 1958). Further specification of the process by Weber is also found in *The Religion of China*, Hans Gerth, trans. and ed. (Glencoe, Ill.: The Free Press, 1951).

5. For one example of large-scale illegal drug transactions, see David Lyle, "The Logistics of Junk," *Esquire Magazine*, March, 1966, pp. 59–67 *passim*.

6. Whether the interpretation is one which prescribes drug use or accepts drug use, drug use as such constitutes a sanctioned means for what stands for the Hippies of the Haight as *their* culturally valued goals. Thus, at least within the Hippie community, those who use drugs are conforming members. Cf. Robert Merton, *Social Theory and Social Structure* (Glencoe, Ill.: The Free Press, 1957, pp. 131–160.

7. Leonard Wolf, *Voices of the Love Generation* (Boston: Little, Brown and Co., 1968), pp. 207–208.

8. *Ibid.*, p. 145–146.

9. *Ibid.*, p. 74.

10. *Ibid.*, p. 135.

11. Chester Anderson and Lorraine Glennby, "Flight Plans," in Jerry Hopkins, ed., *The Hippie Papers* (New York: Signet Books, 1968), p. 68.

12. Wolf, *op. cit.*, p. 51.

13. A similar example of variant interpretations of "good music" can be found in Anthony Burgess, *Clockwork Orange* (New York: Signet Books), where the protagonist recounts how he would listen to Beethoven as a means of evoking fantasies of fights, bloodied bodies, and general violent destruction.

14. There is no way to estimate what proportion of the members

of the community use drugs, in part because there is no precise way to determine the actual population of the community: members are quite frequently coming and going. When members of the community talk about themselves, one of the things they say is "We all use drugs." This may be a matter of members' perception of their own beliefs, or a matter of members' perception of their own practices, or both. However, since the ideologically sanctioned vision need not be obtained by means of drugs, drug use need not be universal in the community. My own observations have included at least two dozen acknowledged members who do not use drugs. But there is no reasonable way to use this figure as a sample of abstinence for the community-at-large.

15. Howard Becker, *Outsiders* (Glencoe, Ill.: The Free Press, 1963), p. 58.

16. *Ibid.*, p. 59.

17. *Ibid.*, pp. 62–78.

18. At least under ordinary circumstances, "freaking-out" (where the drug experience does not go well), extensive trouble with the police, extensive contact with non-drug users, and use of non-drug means of achieving the visionary state may make the interpretative framework and the congruent morality problematic at some subsequent time.

19. Cf. Michael Polanyi, *Personal Knowledge* (New York: Harper Torchbooks, 1964), p. 56. Polanyi makes the general point of "subsidiary awareness" constituting "knowing how" and focal awareness constituting "knowing what." Thus, in effect, matters of subsidiary awareness may be transposed into matters of focal awareness when they are brought in as elements of plans of action. See in this respect, George Miller, et al., *Plans and the Structure of Behavior* (New York: Holt, Rinehart, and Winston, 1960).

20. Charles Frake, "How to Ask for a Drink in Subanum," in *Ethnography of Communication, American Anthropologist* Vol. 66, pt. 2 (1964), pp. 127–132.

21. A similar example of "street dealer" activity in the Midwest can be found in "Confessions of a Campus Pot Dealer," *Esquire Magazine,* September, 1967, pp. 100–101 *passim.*

22. An analogous example of collective attempts to "discern reality" on the part of people in the same situation can be found in Julius Roth, *op. cit.*, pp. 1–20.

23. This same kind of procedure for changing a course of action when "reasonable grounds for justifying it" come up can be seen in

the conventional community as well. In 1966, when it became public knowledge in San Francisco that property taxes would go up substantially on the basis of the new assessment criteria, the "Letters to the Editor" column of the newspaper carried numerous accounts of landlords who "raised their rents to cover their new tax costs" even before the new tax costs were mailed out from the Assessor's Office.

24. "Gold" or "Acapulco Gold" is often used as a generic term for any "fine quality" marijuana. Members will sometimes say that an "even better quality" marijuana is "Panama Red," although during the course of my observations, "Gold" was the most frequently employed term. However, what marijuana is called is not necessarily related to its place of origin, as the following example from field observations indicate:

> Four dealers have been sitting around, idly reminiscing about work. At one point Sam mentions that he is going to see about some "icebag grass." No one else asks him about it, and since it is the first time I have heard the term, I finally ask what "icebag grass" is. Sam answers, "Somebody got some good grass —where a little turned you right on. So they told someone else it was 'icebag grass' to make an extra $20–$25 on it."

25. A similar example can be found on the part of household domestic workers, who have one hourly price for "people they like to work for" and a somewhat higher hourly price which they tell "people they like to work for" to quote to any prospective employer.

26. This is, of course, how the professional thief must also learn to see the conventional culture if he is successfully to practice his chosen career. Cf. David Maurer, *The Big Con* (New York: Signet Books, 1962), and Edwin Sutherland, *The Professional Thief* (Chicago: Phoenix Books, 1958).

27. For descriptions of transaction units in various "drug scenes" see "Mapping the Varieties of Innocence from Antioch to Bob Jones," *Esquire Magazine,* September, 1967, p. 102.

28. This is formally the same for the embezzler, who, in his learning how to detect fraud learns the procedures necessary to engage in it as well. Cf. Donald Cressy, *Other People's Money* (Glencoe, Ill.: The Free Press, 1953), pp. 78–92.

29. In the course of the ongoing activity, it is never weighed, nor is the amount even talked about. Rather, it is generated by a particular visual mass which, if called upon to "estimate," members will speak of as "half an ounce." In the course of learning to live in the

Haight, one also learns to have an "eye" for such matters. A similar kind of visual estimate of quantity can be found in the Indian market-places of the Sierras of Peru. Cf. Frances Toor, *Three Worlds of Peru* (New York: Crown Publishers, 1949), p. 80.

30. Whenever grass is being smoked, it is considered proper and fitting that the joint be offered to anyone who is there. There is no requirement, however, that it be accepted; one can decline by simply saying "no" or shaking one's head when it is offered. Abstinence carries no particular stigma. First, some bona-fide members of the community who are committed to activities such as meditation believe in principle that one should achieve aesthetic states by will and concentration alone, and their beliefs are sanctioned by others who may not share them. Similarly, since "bad trips" on drugs are always a possibility (cf. Chap. 6) and since they can take place for a number of different reasons, it is assumed that any participant who declines the offer of the joint does so for "good reasons," which are treated as personal matters not to be questioned. Occasionally, when a joint is being passed, members may claim to be "high already" or "high on something else," and since being "high" is an eminently personal state, the statement is taken at face value by others. The only time declining the offer of a joint seems to be problematic is when there are only two people present. On all of the occasions that I have been with just one other member and declined to share a lit joint, the other has simply put it out. In these situations it has not been an issue of the other's assumption that I disapprove (since all of them had been with me in larger groups where grass had been smoked). Rather, what seems to be implied is that, like eating in front of others who are not eating in the conventional community, smoking grass when others are not smoking is considered rude. The "rudeness" in the Hippie community is allocated, not to the one who desires to engage in the activity, but to the one who has declined to engage.

31. Cf. Tom Burns, "Friends, Enemies and the Polite Fiction," *ASR,* Vol. 18 (1953), pp. 654–662, and James Woodard, "The Role of Fictions in Cultural Organizations," *Transactions of the New York Academy of Sciences,* Series II, Vol. 6 (June, 1944). pp. 311–344.

32. I have not systematically solicited such gifts and then weighed them in order to compare them with "laid grass" weights. Nor have I been willing to ask others to compare on scales what they get through each mode, since the ideological structure that the transactions take place in makes concern about issues such as precise measure-

ment taboo. However, in the instances which I have observed, there seemed to be somewhat of a difference between the visual mass presented with grass which had been "laid" on someone and grass which has been "requested."

# 7

## The Recognition of Trouble

No matter what members know and expect about the routine properties of everyday life, one of the common contingencies of their
lives is "trouble." While members may anticipate the prospects
of their transactions in "scoring" and "dealing" on ideological
grounds, every member also knows that a transaction of "good
prospects" may turn out to be "a burn" (a bad deal) after all.

The ideology of any group characteristically provides an
idealized version of the world. Ideological beliefs *about* the world
are not actual events, but typifications that members use in antici-
pating actual events and standards for interpreting actual events.
It is in this sense that the ideology of a group provides members
with an interpretative framework for their understanding of the
actual events they encounter. However, as the ideology only constitutes an idealized version of their world, one of the experiences
members actually encounter is "trouble." [1] "Trouble" is any instance where what a member warrantably anticipates and what he
actually encounters demonstrate a perceivable discrepancy. "Trouble" is thus a disjunction between the members' ideological anti-

cipation of what "life should be" and the actual events they encounter. For the members of any group, then, the experience of "trouble" is a possible contingency of their everyday life.

However, not all "trouble" is the same. The first type of "trouble" we may consider "normal trouble." [2] This type involves perceivable discrepancies between what is anticipated and what is encountered that are ideologically understood by members as commonplace matters. "Normal trouble" is what all but the most idealistically naïve members of a group understand life must include.

The second type of "trouble" is "real trouble." "Real trouble" involves perceivable discrepancies between anticipated and encountered events that are seen by members as consequential matters, matters which are likely to generate even more trouble in their wake. [3] Thus, in contrast to "normal trouble," "real trouble" constitutes matters about which something special must be done if the ordinary business of living one's everyday life is to be continued in a perceivably normal fashion. [4]

Members' designation of what will constitute "normal trouble" for them and what will constitute "real trouble" for them is not a matter of simple frequency. There are some groups, e.g., skid row alcoholics, [5] juvenile delinquents, [6] as well as some Hippies of the Haight (such as dealers), for whom "real trouble" may be almost as frequent as "normal trouble." Thus, the analytic distinction between "normal trouble" and "real trouble" rests on members' understanding of the subsequent implications of some discrepancy between what they anticipate and what they encounter. The observable difference between "normal trouble" and "real trouble" is whether members warrantably believe that it is reasonable to ignore it or to engage in corrective action. [7] For the Hippies of the Haight, "a hassle" constitutes "normal trouble," and "a bummer" is "real trouble." "Hassles," once they are acknowledged as such, are characteristically dropped; "bummers" are ordinarily associated with some form of management activity.

SEEING TROUBLE

The Hippies of the Haight are self-consciously ideological;
but the experienced members are not naïvely idealistic, as new recruits to the community often are. As the new recruit (who typically comes to the community with some comprehension of its
ideological tenets) learns how to live everyday life in the Haight,
he learns how to give due consideration to a variety of relevant
factors. In the beginning, the new recruit appears to treat the
ideology as a whole, not as a summation of specific aspects which
can be taken into consideration as they are relevant. But until he
learns to do the latter, his perspective is narrow, or to use analogous terms, "sophomoric" or "idealistic." [8]

This distinction between being ideologically self-conscious
and being naïvely idealistic can be observed in a number of conversations involving older, more experienced members. On at least
five or six occasions, on Haight Street, older members have said to
me as a kind of "comment on the passing scene": "They're all
so young." "Young" in these situations does not seem to be a
members' description of the actual chronological age of the observed others (who frequently appeared about the same age as
the "older" member-commentator). Rather, implied on these occasions was that there seemed to be an extraordinary number of
apparent Hippies on the street. This appearance of numbers on
the street seemed to suggest that there would be an influx of new
—and hence "younger"—members into the community who in
turn would then have a lot to learn. Similarly, the explicit concern
of old members who anticipated an immense influx of potential
members in the summer of 1967 was expressed on numerous
occasions as "It's going to be a bad scene. They (the new recruits)
aren't going to know how to live."

Presumably, at some point or other, new recruits also recognize the distinction between being ideologically self-conscious and
being naïvely idealistic. In some cases, as in the following field

example, the new recruit is shown by the old member that there are in fact ideological distinctions to be made in the expectations of what one is "due" as a Hippie.

> I have taken a car full of Hippies from the Diggers' Free Store to the Town Hall Meeting. During the course of the ride, Fred and Kevin mention that this is their "first day in the Haight." One of the others responds by saying he has been here three months; another says he doesn't even remember when he came.
>
> The Town Hall Meeting has been an attempt by the residents in the area to bring together what they refer to as "members of the New Community" and "members of the Old Community."
>
> During the meeing I sit with the group from the car. At one point, one of the members of the Old Community has the floor. He is talking about purchasing trees to plant along the streets in the District (something which has been of concern on the part of the old residents for as long as I have been here). The speaker urges everybody to contribute or help raise money for the project, and then mentions how much they presently have for it. To this statement of the speaker, Kevin says in a rather loud voice, "They should give that money to the Hippies. They should give that money to us to eat." In response, one of the older members who had been in the car says, directly to Kevin, "You're not hungry yet, are you?"

In other cases, the new recruits may apparently make the discovery of the distinction on their own. Examples of this can be seen in the following two field excerpts, the first one coming from a coffee house, the second from the street.

> I have been talking casually with a Hippie about nothing in particular. At one point he mentions that he has been in the District only a few days. He then goes on to say, "It's not exactly what I expected to find, but I guess I'll stay."

> It has been an extraordinarily warm spring evening and the street has been packed with people: Hippies, young Black adolescents, tourists. The large mixed crowd has generated an aura of tenseness, what the Hippies call "bad vibrations." Two or three people have mentioned it to me as such at the coffee house.
>
> Earlier in the evening there has been a "riot" at Playland (an

amusement park about five miles from the Haight) involving some indeterminate number of Black adolescents. Around eleven o'clock, as I am standing at the corner of Haight and Ashbury, a group of five or six Black adolescents break the plate glass window of the Straight's men's clothing shop on the corner.

By now there is a good deal of anxious milling by the Hippies in the area in general. One of them comes up to me and says, "I have to get off the street. I need a pad to crash. Do you have one?" I say no, and he goes on, in a very anxious tone of voice: 'I just got here. I heard it was a beautiful scene. This isn't what I expected to find. The street is bad." He finally goes off, and I watch him going up to some of the others, presumably making the same request.

Given his immediate reaction to the scene (which was by far the worst situation to that date on the street) one would have expected him to leave the area. However, I saw him on the street two or three weeks later and continued to see him occasionally for some months.

As long as the new recruit is naïvely idealistic—as long as he treats the ideological tenets as *literal* descriptions of the way everything is in the Haight—his everyday life in the Haight is problematic for him. He cannot yet "understand" what practical activities are all about.[9] And as long as he cannot yet "understand" what the practical activities of everyday life in the Haight are all about, he cannot yet "see" trouble.

Thus, for members of the Hippie community, to "see" trouble requires that one first learn how to recognize the practical activities that are to be taken as "life as usual in the Haight." Once this can be done, in effect, life becomes more relaxed.[10]

## KNOWING REAL TROUBLE

Members who can properly translate the ideological tenets of the group into ongoing courses of successful practical activities are able to see "real trouble" when it happens. The experiential knowledge of the members—what they now recognize as being "what usually takes place around here," "the familiar scene of everyday life in the Haight," "how things routinely turn out in practice,"—can be taken into consideration to provide the members with the background against which any kind of trouble (normal or real) can be seen. For the members, the incongruity between an event and their knowledge of what a usual event "looks like"—has looked like in the past—provides grounds for the judgment of trouble. However, any further judgment of what they have encountered, as either "a hassle" or "a bummer," requires that members review the relevant ideological tenets of the group to decide how consequential the incongruity is.

Let us consider the members' problem of "knowing trouble" in terms of general areas of everyday life in which "trouble" may exist for them. This consideration will facilitate both the description of what trouble is for the Hippies of the Haight, and the analysis of how the members make interpretations that result in their distinguishing "hassles" from "bummers." Thus "trouble" for the Hippies of the Haight will be viewed in three general areas of everyday activity: The maintenance of one's body; the maintenance of one's psyche; and the maintenance of one's community. By "maintenance" what I shall consider are those requirements perceived by the members as minimally adequate to continue one's everyday life. Maintenance requirements are thus the dividing line between what members speak of as "unsuccessful living" and what they speak of as "successful living." "Living well" in the Haight generally constitutes a further elaboration on successful living. How one "lives well" includes within it a variety of preferential options, such as the particular kinds of activities one might choose to emphasize in one's life, the style of life one might choose to develop.[11] But how one can live well in the Haight is a less crucial problem than how one successfully lives.

## 1. Maintaining One's Body

Within the Hippie community, one's body is ideologically defined as a thing of beauty in and of itself. The idea that it is merely the corporeal container for one's soul or psyche is largely irrelevant. For the Hippies of the Haight, one has a body and one has a psyche. These two matters are not further considered in terms of their existence as subsidiary elements of some larger entity, such as a-person-composed-of-body-and-soul-together.

Insofar as the body is ideologically defined as a thing of beauty, the basic concern in the behavior of members about their bodies tends to focus more on the outside than on the inside. This means that priority tends to be given to action which will effect the outside rather than the inside when questions arise concerning the undertakings of practical courses of action. As a general rule, then, if a Hippie desires clothing or a string of beads and also desires something to eat, he is likely to choose the former, if he can financially afford only one or the other. Within the Hippie community this is by no means considered an irrational choice on his part. It is not merely the belief that the body is a work of art that gives a member the ideological justification to choose what can be draped on it over what can be put into it. His general knowledge of his world also includes the knowledge that the moral maxim of sharing (derived from the tenets of spiritual community) is a pivotal element in the world as he and other members know it. And he further knows that as a matter of practical activity, others in his world are more likely to act upon this tenet in terms of sharing food than in terms of sharing clothing or baubles, since they too share with him the same set of priorities generated by the community belief about the body as an aesthetic object.[12]

Further support for members' activities is provided by beliefs in the Hippie community about the encompassing Straight society. By and large, as the Hippies "understand" the Straight society, the members of that society are not in harmony with nature and hence are "lost." One can try to demonstrate to the members of the Straight society what the good life is all about by living that life yourself. But the members of the Straight society are understood to be "uptight" (tense and anxious about the life they are living) and hence they are rarely open to comprehending the good life, much less embarking upon it. With a kind of Marxian logic then, the Hippies see the Straight society as having the seeds of its own destruction built right into it.[13]

The implication of this belief about the Straight society (in terms of practical action) is that, since the members of the Straight society are doomed anyway, their life need not be taken into consideration as a matter to respect: it is not a real life because it will not continue. Thus, for example, any opportunity to shoplift from Straight merchants constitutes a reasonable action.[14] However, in the community the distribution of shops between Straight merchants and Hip merchants is generally the same as the distribution between commodities that will feed the body and commodities that will decorate the body. Shoplifting from Hip merchants is, of course, in direct contradiction to the ideological tenets. Whenever it happens, it is always negatively evaluated in members' conversatons with one another. Further, Hip merchants frequently put notices on their windows stressing that the store is both managed and owned by members of the Hippie community; they not infrequently include a reminder that no "real Hippie" would shoplift from his "own" community.

In effect then, if one has money it is eminently reasonable to use it to buy clothing or jewelry rather than food. This means, essentially, that not having food at any particular moment is at most a "hassle"—something that can be expected to pass in the ordinary course of subsequent events, either when one encounters a friend who has food he will share, or when one encounters the opportunity to shoplift it from the Straight merchants.

At the same time, the members of the Hippie community are aware that not having food "right now" is not the same as not having food now and later as well. On the basis of their experiential knowledge they know "some" food is always available. But they also know that fully understanding the moral maxim of sharing is to understand that always receiving and never giving food is likely to cause them to be defined as "bad" Hippies. As they discuss such activities as shoplifting with one another, they also note that the opportunities for shoplifting from Straight merchants are at the most occasional; and extensive shoplifting activities are also likely to cause them trouble with the police. Thus, not having the *prospects* for food stands, for the Hippies of the Haight, as "a bummer," real trouble to be managed.[15]

For members of the community the problem of shelter is one which routinely fluctuates between normal trouble and real trouble.[16] When the weather is good (in San Francisco, good weather is neither predictable nor frequent) not having shelter at any given time is at most normal trouble. The two parks provide an abundance of niches in which to sleep. Since most possessions of the Hippie are those which can be draped over his body or packed in a rucksack, baggage need not be an issue.

The ideological tenet of spiritual community, as it has been translated into practical action over time, has also resulted in members' expectations that friends' pads are open to them for at least the night. It has also resulted in the establishment of numerous communes in the community where shelter is available. Having friends or having addresses thus easily solves the problem of shelter for one night and often for several nights.

Although having money is ideologically without value in and of itself, it is recognized as a potential solution for almost any kind of maintenance problem. The members of the Hippie community recognize that in matters relating to food, shelter, medicine, and drug supply they are not a self-contained community. They understand that at least for the time being— until, as they occasionally put it, "The rest of the city is liberated" —the conventional tokens of exchange are relevant matters in their life. For some, money regularly comes from continued family allowances (and sometimes even money to stay away from home, in the classic "remittance man" style). For others there is remunerative work, either in terms of a business on the street, a craft, peddling papers, or a Straight job.

However, while having money is seen as a potential solution for a variety of maintenance problems, not having money is usually treated as "a hassle"—normal trouble. The ideological definition of money as a meaningless object in and of itself thus fits into the general ideological framework in such a way that not having a regular source of income is never really serious: someone always has some, and can be expected to share either what he actually has, or the means of obtaining it. In this latter case, this means that sources of employment (such as jobs delivering mail for the Post Office) may be shared in and of themselves. One member may go through the formalities of obtaining the job, and share the work of making rounds on a day-to-day basis with others. Eventually, the income produced from the job is shared in the same way. Although I have no direct knowledge of it, members have occasionally mentioned in their conversations the sharing of money on the part of groups of Hippie entrepreneurs (shopkeepers or musicians, for example). As the members have explained it, these groups, by virtue of their actual income, have the possibility of sharing equitably with others and in fact do so.

"Trouble on the job," in terms of any kind of dissatisfaction or boredom, is virtually always treated as "a hassle." It is simply accepted as one of the normal vicissitudes of life while one is working and forgotten about when one is not at work. Or the job is resigned from there and then, since the restrictions required by gainful employment are in direct conflict with the moral maxim of "do your own thing." Thus, "trouble on the job," (which in the conventional society is often treated as a major form of "real trouble") is typically judged by the Hippies of the Haight as limited in its consequences.

## 2. *Maintaining One's Psyche*

In terms of the Hippie ideology, it is within one's psyche or consciousness that one really lives. The ideological tenet of revering and expanding one's consciousness is pivotal, justifying not only drug use as a means of accomplishing this end, but also a variety of other courses of action, such as "doing your own thing," not "blowing your mind" or somebody else's mind (essentially, not being irritated by or irritating to others),[17] and engaging in whatever there is to become engaged in at the moment (e.g., dances, happenings, sitting in the sun, going to the country).

However, on a day-to-day basis, the maintenance of one's psyche tends to produce more "real trouble" than the maintenance of one's body. When the possibility exists for undertaking a course of action which will result in the maintenance of the body or in the maintenance of the psyche, the value priority emphasizes the latter. This means, for example, that just as the con-man takes his security money "off the top of the nut"[18] so too is the Hippie likely to take his psychic maintenance money first out of whatever he has available. That a Hippie of the Haight distributes his available monetary supply for drugs, admission tickets to dances, musical instruments, water pipes, roach holders, kaleidoscopes, posters, buttons, and the like before he addresses the problem of what he will eat or where he will sleep is again, within the ideological structure of the group, not considered irrational.

As the Hippies of the Haight explain the issue, if one's psyche is not stimulated, one is simply not alive, regardless of the particular condition of one's physiological state. In terms of the beliefs of the group, the aesthetic decoration of the body contributes to the stimulation of one's psyche. But in the last analysis, while such decoration is viewed as necessary to stimulation, it is not sufficient. Furthermore, since the psychic life is understood to be a *very* immediate thing, not a matter to be considered for some future time, psychic whims are to be acted upon immediately, when they come. This sense of immediacy results in a drastic foreshortening of the sense of the present when what is involved is the maintenance of the psyche. One has to have what one desires right now; postponement is pain. Thus what is required to maintain the psyche must be contained within the boundaries of the here and now.

In a word, any time one wants to dance and cannot enter the auditorium, any time one wants a trip-toy (e.g., kaleidoscope, candles, posters, bells) and does not have it, any time one wants a crowd of happy people and there is not one, is treated as an occasion that must be managed. Such times are occasions that are to be defined as, in effect, "bummers."

Insofar as one's psyche is understood as being, in the last analysis, entirely one's own problem, psychic irritation which is produced by the activities of other people is frequently defined as "a hassle." While it is understood that the social presence of other members of the community can successfully contribute to one's psychic maintenance, their company is not sufficient. In this sense, just as one's sense of the present is foreshortened when one is considering matters of the psyche, so too are one's definitions of social relationships foreshortened to matters with no more than immediate implications.[19]

As a matter of practical, everyday action, this means that when members are "put up tight" by the behavior of others (made psychically uncomfortable) they simply "quit the scene." In some instances this may involve telling the other outright, "Stop blowing my mind," or "You're bringing me down." They may also socially "turn the other off" (i.e., studiously ignore him), or just physically leave the setting without saying anything.

This adaptation results in a situation where social relationships, as they are characteristically understood in the conventional world, take on the appearance of being shallow, erratic, tentative, and sometimes non-existent.[20] However, within the ideological framework of the Hippie community, a "relationship" is not something which is defined in terms of its long-range consequences, specified rights and obligations, or an extended system of deference and demeanor. Rather, a "relationship" is to be considered to be "meaningful" if the participants "groove together" at any one time. By this is meant simply that they are "psychically compatible." And as members describe it, this compatibility is to be known when they do not experience psychic irritation from the other.

In terms of everyday activity, then, psychic irritation produced by the behavior of other members is treated largely as normal trouble. This understanding is possible since the very actions which serve to maintain the psyche (e.g., quitting the scene) serve to solve the problem of irritation there and then. If, for example, one walks out on a friend without saying anything to him, it is understood that no apology or any other kind of reconciliatory activity will be subsequently required when they encounter one another again. Thus, since nothing is required to re-establish the relationship, there is in effect no management problem.

Since for members drug use is an ideologically justified means of maintaining one's psyche, anything related to that experience can potentially generate trouble. Occasions of trouble over drug use are often spoken of as "a bummer" (whereas trouble in obtaining drugs is more likely to be spoken of as "a hassle"). Most observed occasions of trouble with respect to drug use involved what members speak of as "having bad trips" (unpleasant experiences while on drugs); "freaking-out" (becoming afraid and/or disorganized both while on drugs and after); and "being busted" (being arrested for the possession of drugs).

With respect to psychic troubles, members in conversation with one another frequently reminisce about "bad trips they have had." In the context of such conversations, such experiences are occasionally spoken of as being "a bum trip" or "a bummer." However, in no observed occasion of their reminiscence on this subject has anything ever been mentioned of the troublesome consequence beyond the experience of the "bum trip." The following field excerpts provide two such examples:

> Paul and George have been talking about hitchhiking. Paul mentions that the last time he hitchhiked to Marin, he was high on acid. He goes on saying, "This Straight cat picked me up at Ramon Street and all the way over he's rapping about how drugs are bad for you, what they do to your mind. That was really a bummer." I ask Paul what he did about it and he answers, "Nothing. What was there to do?"
>
> George then says he prefers to hitch a ride with other Hippies because "then you don't have to hassle with sermons."

> Sue has been talking about the evening she and some others spent at the Avalon Ballroom. She goes on to explain that after they left the auditorium, she and two others (who were high on

acid) tried to cross the street, became disorganized, and just stood in the middle of the street "for what seemed to be an hour." She goes on to add, "What a bummer that was. I thought we would be there for the rest of our lives." The story concludes rather undramatically, with the group finally getting across the street, catching a bus, and returning home in what seemed to be a normal fashion.

Thus, for the Hippies of the Haight, while a "bad trip" may occasionally be referred to as a "bum trip" or "a bummer" such experiences tend to be ultimately treated as though they were limited in their consequences. In contrast, both "freaking-out" and "being busted" are not only matters talked about with great animation among members, but in such conversations, elaborate specification is often made of the set of subsequent activities the experiences involve. Raising bail, having a date set to go to court, and occasionally even spending time in jail are, for the members, all known consequences of "being busted." Furthermore, "being busted" is not only real trouble for the members, but real trouble of a very special sort: one which takes them out of their community without their desire to leave, and one that links them up with institutions of the conventional society without their desire to be linked. Thus, in most observed conversations about "being busted," the reminiscence by one member of his own experiences frequently generates further general discussion. Such discussions involve other members recounting their experiences of "being busted," and they characteristically involve descriptions of the experiences of others they have known.[21] In contrast to "bad trips," which are only occasionally referred to as being "a bummer," "being busted," is always spoken of in this way.

Finally, unlike "bad trips," "freaking-out," is not only treated as real trouble, but in many respects tends to be treated by the Hippies of the Haight as the worst kind of trouble they can encounter. This appears to be not so much a matter of its being unmanageable trouble, but rather it is an experience which their belief system denies as a possibility. "Freaking-out" differs from simply a "bad trip." As the members understand it, the drug experience contributes either directly or indirectly to a successful "expansion" of one's psychic consciousness. The psyche contains all that is real, pleasurable, and beautiful in the universe. A "bad trip" is a drug experience which is somewhat less than beautiful or somewhat less than pleasurable. In contrast, one has "freaked out" not merely when what one encounters is discrepant with this ideological description, but when what one encounters has the appearance of being a direct contradiction of what one is led to expect and when there is no apparent ideological justification for the experience. Thus, while "bad trips" can be explained (e.g., the wrong setting, the wrong company, the wrong frame of mind) "freaking-out" is ideologically senseless.

### 3. Maintaining One's Community

Occasionally members make projections of what the Hippie community will be like when it reaches its full fruition. What is usually involved is a description of an immense communal collectivity, where each member, doing his own thing, experiences no restrictions on his own activity, feels no oppression from any organized society—their own or others—and has, in the meantime, realized all the beauty and truth of the universe. As they say, "That's what it's (the Hippie movement) all about." With this state seen as the teleological end, the present community in the Haight is usually referred to as its beginning. The discrepancies which take place on a community-wide level are not seen as real trouble, since these are the things that anyone would expect when something "radical and important" is just beginning to happen.

What this means, in effect, is that for all practical purposes, the maintenance of their community requires no particular management by the members, and, by and large, is accorded no management treatment. Members simply understand that "eventually it will all change on its own." Anything that any particular member, or any collectivity of members, may do is not considered activities undertaken for the maintenance of the community. Rather, it is simply understood as the particular member's "thing."

It must be quite clear here that, as noted in the section on methodology, I have little direct observational data on the numerous communes which have existed in the District. Some members consider the communes to be "limited communities," i.e., small scale models of what the general communty will eventually be like. When members talk to one another about their own experiences in communes, with very few exceptions, their accounts do not vary from the ideological description of what communal life should be like. Occasionally in such member-conversations, mention will be made of the disruptive activity of other member-residents, who "do not live up to the ethical precepts of sharing." Sometimes the referent of "sharing" is goods, possessions, and space; other times it is responsibility for keeping the commune going. In a few accounts members have mentioned leaving communes because of restrictions on privacy they impose, explaining that this restriction on privacy has resulted in a restriction on individual freedom as well.[22]

Leaving the question of the communes—as small scale models of the community—aside, then, the Hippie community at large in the Haight, in terms of everyday practices, tends to be treated as much more a collectivity of like-minded persons than a group which binds the participants together in a network of fixed rights and obligations. Real trouble by and large does not exist with reference to problems of maintaining the community per se, but only with reference to maintaining individual members *in* the community. What this results in, essentially, is that community management activities are required only as matters of response to another member's request for help with his real troubles—as we shall see in the next chapter, with its focus on how members who have "real troubles" manage them.

In summary, for all but the naïvely idealistic members of the community, experiences which are discrepant with what they ideologically expected to encounter are characteristically distinguished in terms of whether they constitute "a hassle" or "a bummer." The former are matters of "normal" and the latter matters of "real" trouble. The distinction between what is to be treated as "a hassle" and what is to be treated as "a bummer" appears to be a matter of both practical experience and ideological relevance, wherein the practical experience of members provides the ground for assessing the ideological implications of the situation. In this sense, members must first be able to judge what "normal events in the Haight" are before they can assess the nature of their experience as either "a hassle" or "a bummer." However, the experience of "bummers" does not necessarily invalidate the beliefs which members hold about the world. Not only are such experiences of "real trouble" defined in terms of the tenets of the Hippie ideology, but the practical management of such trouble is sanctioned in ideologically-relevant terms as well.

## NOTES

1. The more practical problem is that of how members encounter anything which they may be seeking in and of itself, or seeking to avoid.

2. Cf. Harold Garfinkel, *Studies in Ethnomethodology* (Englewood Cliffs, N.J.: Prentice-Hall, 1967), pp. 186–207, David Sudnow, "Normal Crimes: Sociological Features of the Penal Code in a Public Defender's Office," *Social Problems,* Vol. 12 (1965), pp. 225–276, and Sherri Cavan, *Liquor License* (Chicago: Aldine Publishing Co., 1966), pp. 67–87.

3. This same distinction is employed by Egon Bittner in "Police Discretion in Emergency Apprehension of Mentally Ill Persons," *Social Problems,* Vol. 14 (1967), pp. 278–292.

4. By and large, the sociological study of trouble has focused on "real troubles" insofar as this constitutes a perceivably-real problem for members of any group. However, Edwin Lemert's distinction of primary and secondary deviance suggests that under some circumstances "normal trouble" may eventually be transformed into "real trouble." See, for example, Lemert's "Paranoia and the Dynamics of

Exclusion," *Sociometry*, Vol. 25 (1962), pp. 2–25; and Thomas Scheff, *Becoming Mentally Ill* (Chicago: Aldine Publishing Co., 1966), pp. 31–54.

5. See, for example, Jacqueline P. Wiseman, *Stations of the Lost* (Englewood Cliffs, N.J.: Prentice-Hall, 1970).

6. Cf. Carl Werthman and Irving Piliavin, "Gang Members and the Police," in D. Bordua, ed., *The Police: Six Sociological Essays* (New York: John Wiley and Sons, 1967), pp. 56–98.

7. This can be seen most explicitly in the area of law, where what is proscribed by law is not only spelled out, but what subsequent action is to be taken once such legal trouble is uncovered is also specified. Cf. H. L. A. Hart, *The Concept of Law* (Oxford: Oxford University Press, 1961).

8. For an example of learning how to engage in practical actions and learning how to see "real trouble" in the area of conventional work, see Howard Becker, "The Career of the Chicago Public School Teacher," *AJS*, Vol. 57 (1952), pp. 470–477, and Howard Becker and Blanch Geer, *Boys in White* (Chicago: University of Chicago Press, 1961).

9. Cf. Garfinkel, *op. cit.*, pp. 35–75 and *passim*. The problem of members "learning to understand" the life their membership entails is treated by Harvey Sacks, "The Search for Help: No One To Turn To," unpublished manuscript, June 23, 1965.

10. Cf. Bittner, "Police Discretion," *op. cit.*, p. 292.

11. An example of analogous preferential options as elaborations on members' perception of basic requirements is provided in David Mandelbaum, "Form, Variation and Meaning of a Ceremony," in R. F. Spencer (ed.), *Method and Perspective in Anthropology* (Minneapolis: The University of Minnesota Press, 1954), pp. 60–102.

12. Cf. George Simmel, *The Sociology of George Simmel* (Glencoe, Ill.: The Free Press, 1950), pp. 338–342, for a general discussion of the role of adornment in social life.

13. This point, along with the beliefs in the freedom of man and the ultimate goal of "community" are common ideological premises for both the Hippies and what has been generally referred to as "The New Left." However, the crucial difference between the two is in the interpretation employed to formulate practical plans for action; and thus, the routine activities the two groups engage in are not always the same. This is not to say that individual membership may not overlap the two, but that even with some ideological congruence, the everyday life of the Hippies of the Haight and the everyday life

of the "New Left" are quite dissimilar. For general descriptions of the "New Left," see, for example, Jack Newfield, *A Prophetic Minority* (New York: Signet Books, 1966), and Students for a Democratic Society, *The Port Huron Statement,* (New York: Students for a Democratic Society, 1964).

14. In conversations taking place between Straight merchants, one of the most frequent remarks to be heard concerns the extent to which shoplifting in the District has increased since the Hippies have been in the area. Similarly, at one of the large supermarkets in the District, the arrival of the paddy wagon, and its departure with one, two, or more apparent Hippies in tow, was observed—sometimes as many as four and five times in one week.

15. Complaints by older members that there is too much panhandling in the area are not infrequent. Much of it is perceived by old members as activity of "teenyboppers"—who are either considered non-members, or new recruits. This seems to be my perception from observations as well. It may be that the "teenybopper"— as a non-experienced member—sees not having goods at any given moment as real trouble rather than normal trouble, and hence is engaged in constant management activity in the form of panhandling money for food. Alternatively, it may be that the "teenybopper" is not a new recruit, but in fact a non-member: one who does not share the general ideology in the first place, and hence one who is not likely to select his practical activities in the same way as old members do.

16. "Shelter" may include an entire apartment or flat, a private room, a private bed, access to an apartment (where exactly one may be able to sleep is to be negotiated), or a truck or bus, as well as public areas such as the parks.

17. To "blow your mind" has two meanings: being irritated and being ecstatic. Its specific referent is not necessarily the situation in which it is spoken, but the tone of voice employed when it is said: disgust for the first meaning; awe for the second.

18. Cf. David Maurer, *Whiz Mob* (New Haven, Conn.: College and University Press, 1964), p. 194.

19. The assumption of inconsequentiality of the setting creates a similar situation with respect to social relationships in bars. Cf. Cavan, *op. cit.,* pp. 49–66.

20. Examples of such descriptions of relationships among the Hippies can be found in "Hippie Generation: Slouching Toward Bethlehem," *Saturday Evening Post,* Vol. 240 (September 23, 1967), pp. 25–31; "Strange New Loveland of the Hippies," *Life,* Vol. 62

(March 31, 1967), pp. 15–16; and "Hippie," *Time,* Vol. 90 (July 7, 1967), pp. 18–22.

21. "Busts" are a constant topic of both gossip and rumor in the community: who has been recently busted in the first case; impending possibilities in the second.

22. I have also heard a few accounts (by both members and observers) of life on the communal farms. In such accounts, what is not infrequently mentioned is that "farming" and "doing your own thing" are not always compatible. In these reports as well, it seems to be that the general solution to the situation is for members to simply leave the farms, and hence seemingly treat the endeavor much like they treat conventional jobs: as normal trouble. Two published accounts of the communal farms can be found in Jerry Hopkins, ed., *The Hippie Papers* (New York: Signet Books, 1968), pp. 23–25, and Leonard Wolf, *Voices of the Love Generation* (New York: Little, Brown and Co., 1968), pp. 105–106.

# 8

## How To Manage Trouble
## in the Haight

By definition, when a member knows he has encountered "real trouble," he knows that somehow it must be managed. However, knowing that "real trouble has to be managed" is not the same as knowing "how to manage real trouble." Part of the commonsense knowledge about the world for the members of *any community* includes the knowledge of how to deal with "trouble" when they meet it. In the conventional world of everyday middle-class American life, normal adult members know that there are various institutionalized agencies (e.g., the police, the doctor, the social worker, city hall, the Better Business Bureau, insurance companies) that manage trouble for other members. In this world, normal adult members also know that agencies specialize in the kind of trouble they will manage. Thus, part of the task of trouble management for the members of the conventional society is identification of the trouble so that members can decide to which particular agency it should be taken. This knowledge is not necessarily complete for everyone within the conventional society. It may be ambiguous to the individual just what his trouble is: for example, piles of garbage may be a sanitation problem for the public health department or a housekeeping problem for the landlord, who should have the garbage taken away. A person within the middle-class American society may also be uncertain about the actual kinds of troubles the particular agencies do in fact manage: for example, does the police system oversee suspected dishonesty in a tradesman's bill, or only theft outside of presumably legitimate business dealings? Finally, there may be a discrepancy between what the lay member of the society defines as his trouble and the definition of it by a professional member of some particular agency. Thus, as one example, the classroom deportment of a child may be considered by the parent a problem to be managed by the school, while the professional members of the school system may see it as a problem to be managed by a psychiatrist.

Furthermore, the identity of the kind of "real trouble" one has encountered in the conventional society affects whether or not it may be taken to certain institutionalized agencies for management. For example, some families are reluctant to call the police to manage family fights; furthermore the police are reluctant to respond to calls to manage them. The appropriate management of this kind of trouble thus depends upon whether what is taking place is identified as a "family fight" or as an instance of "mental illness" in one of the family members. Until such an identification is settled, the appropriate action to be taken to resolve the trouble is problematic.

In one sense, conventional American society is noteworthy for the proliferation of institutionalized agencies for the management of members' troubles. There are police to manage troubles stemming from damage to person and property; physicians to manage troubles of bodily illness; dentists to manage teeth troubles; psychiatrists to take care of the mind; city hall to manage civic rights; the Better Business Bureau to manage fair market exchange; and insurance companies to manage trouble from losses. In addition, there are adoption agencies to manage the problem of wanting a child—or not wanting a child; lonely hearts clubs for problems of finding a mate; marriage counselors for problems of living with one's mate; employment agencies for problems of finding a job; vocational counselors for problems of working at a job; travel agents for problems of what to do when you have a vacation from the job, and on and on and on.

There is clearly a plethora of institutionalized agencies to manage any conceivable instance of real or potential troubles the members of conventional society may encounter. Yet a separate and distinct matter for members of the conventional society is whether he is, in fact, to take his "real trouble" to an agency for its management or not. The ideological tenet of "self-reliance" in the middle-class segment of the conventional world results in the general understanding that, if one wants to maintain one's sense of self-integrity, there are many kinds of "real trouble" one must attempt to manage oneself. In effect, a parent who can control his child only with the help of a child guidance counselor is, if this fact were known, to be considered differently from a parent who can control his child himself. What troubles members are automatically to take to agencies for help in their management and what troubles they should attempt to manage themselves seems to be variable for different segments of the conventional world. Thus again, the sanctioned identification of "what" kind of trouble one has becomes important in deciding whether it should be taken to an appropriate agency or managed on the part of the member himself.

But the point of this survey of trouble management agencies is that within the everyday conventional world, there tends to be some institutionalized service to manage whatever "real trouble" members either do not wish to or cannot manage themselves.

Everyday life in the Hippie community stands in contrast to these arrangements within the conventional community. Members of the Hippie community characteristically refer to the management of their "real troubles" as their own individual problem. There are ideologically grounded "good reasons" for this view. The ideological tenet of "free expression of the self" along with the moral maxim: "Do your own thing" characteristically creates almost impenetrable barriers to any kind of long-run, community-organized endeavor. Collective enterprises do exist, but they depend upon the whims of members. Such enterprises are maintained only as long as they involve what each individual participant-qua-individual wants to do. These barriers to ongoing organized endeavors which would in general support the way of life of the Hippie community are further reinforced by the ideological tenet of revering and expanding one's own consciousness. This tenet, as noted in the previous chapter, results in the same kind of practical action as the tenet of the "free expression of the self." Specifically, members *want* to do only what gives them psychic satisfaction to do *at the moment*. And, as suggested in Chapter 3, the ideological tenet of the spiritual community of man does not postulate self-abnegation, or its corollary, self-denial. Rather, it simply puts forth an ethic of sharing when it is apparent that one *can* share. Such a view does not encourage "the spirit of give and take" required for stable concerted action.

There have been, between 1966 and 1968, a number of institutions for the management of trouble within the Haight. These agencies have included the Diggers' Free Store, the Diggers' provision of free food, a Free Medical Clinic, the Job-Co-op, Project Life Line (a referral system to available agencies in the community-at-large), Huckleberry House (for youthful runaways), Happening House (as a kind of community center), and the Council for the Summer of Love (a project to assist with the influx of new members anticipated in the summer of 1967). Also, at one time the Communication Company (a publishing enterprise) put out a handbook for survival on the street. Some of these management institutions have been completely indigenous to the Hippie community; some of them have been established with the assistance of outside volunteers. However, the characteristic feature of most of these organizations has been their generally short life-span and ideologically tenuous position in the Hippie community. While they have been *utilized* by members involved in managing their troubles, their actual maintenance by members as a collective enterprise is always problematic. The moral maxim of "Do your own thing" can result in collective community endeavors; but it cannot guarantee the continued existence of those endeavors over time once they have begun. For the maxim suggests that other alternatives may easily replace the collective endeavor and that they are socially sanctioned as replacements. There is no "support your local agency" drive in the Hippie community. Thus, by and large, while various institutionalized means of managing members' troubles have existed at various times in the community, during the ongoing course of my observations, they have not been the *typical* ways for members to manage the troubles they experience.

As a result, the Hippies, taken collectively and in general, appear to demonstrate a greater extent of "self-reliance" on a day-to-day basis than do the members of the conventional society, taken in the same way. But the Hippies are "self-reliant" for reasons of ideological considerations that are quite different from those in the conventional world. In the conventional community, "self-reliance" is an ideological virtue; for the Hippies of the Haight, it is a fact of life.

In order to live out one's everyday life in the Hippie community successfully, members must be able to know "real trouble" when they see it. And, just as important, they must know the sanctioned means to manage it once they have seen it. In the following sections the concern will be "how to manage trouble in the Haight." Again, what shall be suggested is that members' understandings of "how to manage trouble in the Haight" is a matter of sanctioned practices, and like the other regular and routine courses of action they engage in, these sanctioned troubles are structured in terms of the ideological tenets they hold.

The sanctioned procedures for the management of "trouble" in the Haight will be considered in terms of three general strategies of management: (1) Preventing: practices whose success is not doubted for preventing trouble; (2) Coping: the active manipulation of alternatives to manage trouble; and (3) Explaining: means of putting trouble in its proper perspective. Which particular strategy is to be selected for the management of any given member's "real trouble" is characteristically treated by members as an idiosyncratic matter. The selection of strategy thus appears to be governed much more by personal preference and opinion than by ideological standards and evaluations of efficiency. For example, evaluation of the particular choice of strategy made by a member has been a topic of dispute in only a few conversations concerning management activity. Furthermore, in observations of occasions when one member has requested information of another about what to do for the management of *his* troubles, the one asked almost always either said, "I don't know," or prefaced his suggestions with, "I don't know. Maybe you could try. . ." The implication of such answers seems to be that while there are sanctioned practices understood as applicable to the management of trouble, no particular practice is sanctioned for any particular trouble.

Although the general strategies tend to be acknowledged as sanctioned practices by the members of the community, there are varied opinions about the particular tactical procedures by which those strategies can be implemented.

## *1. Preventing*

For the members of any group, the management of their troubles by preventive practices is not a matter of simply managing to avoid trouble altogether. Rather, what members in general understand as "preventive practices" are courses of action which are undertaken in advance of encountering any particular trouble. The efficacy of such practice is not doubted, even if trouble is subsequently encountered. For example, in the conventional world, members' understanding of "preventive practices" to avoid colds may include such activities as keeping fit, getting the proper rest, eating the proper diet, protection from undue exposure to the elements, and even taking a large dose of vitamin C every day. But accepting this array of "preventive practices" does not imply that believers never get colds. Rather, it implies that persons who engage in these practices do not doubt their efficaciousness despite the existence of deviant cases (catching cold). Once one believes in a set of "preventive practices" and acts upon them, one understands the world in terms of their effectiveness: i.e., one has had fewer colds a year than one *would have had* if one had not undertaken such "preventive practices" in the first place. In conventional middle-class American society, the logic of "preventive practices" can be seen even more clearly in respect to beliefs about dental hygiene: one brushes one's teeth at least twice a day to prevent cavities; and then one goes to the dentist twice a year for management of those cavities one develops anyway.

Thus, the essential character of "preventive practices" is that they are believed to be effective and that they involve the management of "real trouble" in advance of its actual occurrence.

Since the belief system of the Hippie community places special stress on members' psyches, most of the "preventive practices" undertaken in the community are practices that are understood to minimize the potential of psychic troubles. Such psychic troubles may cover such phenomena as the inability of one's consciousness to grasp the ideologically "true" reality of the world and the inability of one's consciousness to contend with the drug experience.

One form of "preventive practices" for some segments of the community is Yoga. There is a commitment to Yoga as a means of preparing one's consciousness to be, in general, receptive to the experiences it will undergo. Yoga teaches one to control the body in such a way that the corporeal person will not interfere with the psychic person. Within the District it is thus not uncommon to find Hippies engaged in Yoga exercises wherever and whenever the opportunity permits. Nor is it uncommon to find other members ignoring those so engaged. For anyone may feel the need for preventive exercise at any time and it is expected that one acts upon the necessity one sees.

Two males, whom I have talked to occasionally in the past about the relationship of Yoga and awareness, are in the park. There are about forty to forty-five Hippies sitting around, some engaged in conversation, some just being. The two males are at the bottom of the slope of the hill, in the direction that most of the others are faced. When I arrive they are both engaged in a convoluted series of Yoga exercises, which continue for almost twenty minutes. Once they have stopped, the two of them sit and talk.

One of the people sitting in the room mentions that she just started on a regime of Yoga exercises "because it helps me think better," although it is never mentioned specifically what is meant by "thinking better."

For some, the practice of Yoga as a "non-Western" method of treating the body can serve as a preparatory method of liberating one's self from the general constraints of the conventional society as well as preparing one's consciousness for liberating new experiences. On a few occasions, Hippies committed to Yoga have stated that were it to be taught as a regular part of the physical education program in the Straight schools, those schools would turn out "fewer mass-produced conformists." A similar understanding of Yoga can be seen in the following excerpts from field observations:

Felix and I are walking through the park when suddenly he falls to his knees, opens his eyes extraordinarily wide, and sticks out his tongue as far as it will go toward his nose. He remains that way for about thirty to forty seconds; then gets up and we continue walking.

I recognize it is the "Lion Position" but say nothing about it then, nor does Felix. Later, when we are talking about what is involved in "being yourself" he says: "In the park, when I went into the Lion Position—I just wanted to. It helps me relax, be free."

I ask him if he often does it in such a sudden and spontaneous way. He replies that he does if that's the way he feels at the moment.

Like Yoga, macrobiotics is understood as constituting daily practices that prevent psychic difficulties. Macrobiotics prevent the corporeal body from negatively influencing the psychic consciousness. The general explanation (which is fairly regularly encountered in the community) is that the organic nature of macrobiotic foods rids the body of toxic properties that are detrimental to the expansion of one's mind. The following field example is typical of such explanations.

> Stella is invited to have dinner with us but refuses because, as she says simply, "I'm on macrobiotics." I ask her whether one ordinary dinner will matter and she goes into an elaborate explanation of "body chemistry" which includes such things as negative discharges produced by contact of "pure foods" (macrobiotic foods) and "impure foods" (what we are serving).

For some committed to the preventive practices of macrobiotics, commitment extends to refusing to eat anyplace where ordinary non-organic food is served, presumably because the "negative reactions" that take place between conventional food and macrobiotic food in the body may take place outside it as well. Although I have not observed such instances directly, three or four members have mentioned knowing someone who will not even enter an establishment where non-organic foods are served.[1] A similar implication concerning such practices of maintaining purity is contained in the following ad for a macrobiotic restaurant in one of the Underground newspapers:

> Clean "Smokeless Air" to breathe
> While—eating and enjoying one's
> refreshment and meals. .
> Mountain Spring "Fluoride Free" water
> used in "Macrobiotic and
> Vegetarian" cooking—in Coffee
> and Herb drinks

The sanction of Yoga on the part of the community-at-large does not, however, extend to macrobiotics. Negative remarks concerning macrobiotics are about as prevalent from some members as the practice of macrobiotics is for other members. Occasionally, members who do not follow a strict macrobiotic diet will serve only macrobiotic foods simply as "a change of diet," as the following field examples note:

> At Loretta's house, where a large, planned-in-advance party is taking place, there are only macrobiotic foods. I ask her about them and she explains that she cooks macrobiotics occasionally for herself and her family "just for a change of menu." However, she goes on to describe the damage that a continued diet of macrobiotics will produce, and evinces concern for those who do not realize this.

> There is a large platter of macrobiotic cookies sitting on the table. I ask the hostess if she made them and she responds that they were made and brought over by someone else who is there. However, her response is very quick, and carries the overtones that she does not particularly approve of macrobiotics generally, though she later acknowledges that these cookies taste very good.

In their preventive dietary practices Hippie community members show little acceptance of methods practiced by members of conventional society who are committed to "health foods." However, there is a somewhat parallel belief that chemical substances used in conventionally prepared food (such as preservatives) are detrimental to health. For the Hippies, as for conventional food faddists, the detrimental effects of chemical substances in foods focuses more on general physical damage than it does on any psychic damage. This focus may account for less widespread interest in dietary rules in the larger Hippie community.

In addition to exercise and diet, "preventive practices" related to the avoidance of psychic difficulties include meditation. For some, such meditation may involve special rooms, music, incense, and other aids. For others, it may involve only the occasional reading of various books on Eastern philosophy. In such cases it is understood that the reflective meditation which prepares the consciousness for expansion is contained in the words of Eastern Sages.

There are also preventive practices concerning drug use.

Within the belief system of the community, the close relationship of the drug experience and the expansion of consciousness provides grounds for engaging in preparations of various kinds prior to the use of drugs.

Such preparatory activities to assure a successful drug experience tend to be much more prevalent in the use of acid, for members consider acid to be one of the most powerful drugs for expanding one's consciousness. The following field examples provide typical illustrations of such practices:

> Six people are sitting around, talking about plans for their prospective "acid trip." Two of the six have not taken acid before and Lloyd is explaining to them how important it is for their first trip to be in the woods (where theirs will be) or by the ocean, or "any place outside of the city."
>
> I ask Lloyd why that is so and he answers that from the experience, you will ultimately realize that you will have to live in harmony with nature. Thus, if you "start your voyage in nature" you will be that much further ahead.
>
> Somewhat later he says to one of the others, "The city is what man has done *to* the earth, not something he's done *with* it."

> Parts of a conversation overheard at one of the tables at the coffee house: the general topic is "dropping acid," and there seems to be some concern about a third person. One of the speakers says something to the effect that this third person isn't "ready to take any acid now," and goes on to say that "he's too much on a power trip now for it to do him any good."

> A group of people sitting in the park, talking about "dropping acid" in general: one of them says, "You should always be in beautiful surroundings and with beautiful people, otherwise it will be a bummer."
>
> I ask if that is true even if one has had a good deal of experience with the drug, and she replies that it is.

For some members, "preventive practices" may focus on managing troubles, other than psychic troubles, in advance. The use of omens as signs indicating what one should or should not do is occasionally encountered.[2] One example is provided by the following excerpt from field observations:

> Beth is talking about how many automobile accidents she has seen in the past few months. She goes on to say, "It's a sign. I know it's a sign for me to leave the city, otherwise I wouldn't be the one to see so many of them."

Thus far we have considered prevention and avoidance of trouble. Let us turn now to more active procedures to manage trouble.

## 2. Coping

"Coping" rests upon the members' perception of the manipulative possibilities of their world: what actions can be undertaken to alter the immediate state of affairs as they are given. "Coping" is intricately related to the belief structure of the group, for what is perceived by members as fixed and what is perceived by them as alterable is not given in nature. Instead, such matters are open to community-sanctioned definition.

"Coping" *per se* is by the definition of the term always open to innovation, as individual members come to formulate new possibilities out of their practical circumstances and the given material of their ideological tenets. Whether any such innovative coping activity by one individual is to be treated as "legitimate and acceptable" on the part of other members rests upon the latter's ability to "see" (comprehend) the concordant relevance of the activity to the ideology on one hand and to the trouble on the other.[3] For such innovative means of coping to be subsequently adopted by other members of the community rests on their acknowledgment that such means are not only sanctionable, but that they work—that they do in fact manage the troubles they were implemented to manage.

However, if such innovative "coping" activities are not initially considered "ideologically acceptable," the pragmatic test is irrelevant. Such activities cannot fall within the scope of what "good members do." Those who utilize ideologically unsanctioned means of coping with their "trouble" provide grounds for others to re-evaluate the rights of the former to the status of member-in-good-standing.

For example, as noted in Chapter 7, "normal trouble" may remain simply "normal trouble" where members solve their immediate lack of food by shoplifting. The problem of "no food now or latter either" may be coped with by shoplifting as well. However, in both instances, shoplifting is sanctioned by the community in general only if it is not done from other members, such as the Hip merchants.

In the present section, I shall be concerned only with ideologically sanctioned coping activities. Furthermore, I shall be concerned only with those ideologically sanctioned coping activities which are generally known to and employed by the Hippies of the Haight as means of managing "real trouble"—activities which constitute a frequent topic of conversation and have been observed on numerous occasions.

The moral maxim of sharing is a precept which both sanctions and makes effective the managing of one's "trouble" by asking for help. It provides the member with grounds to believe that he has the right to ask and grounds to believe that other members are likely to comply. In fact, asking is probably the most ubiquitous means of coping in the community. It is not restricted to asking only other members, however.

As the following excerpts from field observations illustrate, members can ask other members for food, for shelter, and for money (as well as for grass, as noted in Chapter 6).

> I am walking down Haight Street with someone I had started talking with at the park, but do not know by name. A girl comes up and asks us if we have any "spare change." Both of us say no. I later ask my companion, "Don't you find it strange when Hippies panhandle from other Hippies?" He answers simply, "No, why shouldn't they?"

> A happening is in progress in the Panhandle. A rather large crowd of Hippies has gathered and eventually a Rock group appears with a flat-bed truck that they use as a stage. Apparently the people in the park had expected the arrival of the group,

since they are met with cheers and a general intensification of the pitch of activity. There is some delay in the setup of the sound equipment. But as soon as it has been tested, the first noise to come across is a pitch on the part of one of the musicians for "donations for bail money" for the members of some other Rock group who had been "busted for possession" (of drugs). A number of people standing around the stage take hats, paper bags, and other suitable containers and start meandering through the crowd, collecting change. Once they have started, the band begins to play. Throughout the afternoon the announcement is made repeatedly, along with the passing of the hat. No announcement is made about how much of the necessary $2000 has been collected; although thanks for contributions are frequently announced publicly.

I am walking down Haight Street eating an orange. Someone steps out from the group lolling against the fronts of the shops and says, "Can I have part of your orange?" I give him half, he nods his thanks, and goes back to where he was.

Three of us are sitting in the park, with a rather large picnic lunch that Julia has prepared. On three occasions other Hippies in the park come by and simply ask, "Can I get something to eat?" Those I am with comply in the same way that the members of conventional society comply with requests from strangers for a match.

Arthur tells me of a Hippie he gave a ride to, who asked Arthur if he had a crash pad as well. Arthur said the other spent the night (as well as eating at his place).

Food, shelter, and money are the requests most frequently made of other members.[4] But these do not exhaust the sanctioned possibilities of coping by asking for help. Like panhandling, hitch-hiking as a request for transportation is common. I have no knowledge of the full range of things that may be in fact requested within the community. My own experiences of having been asked (as a perceived member of the community) have included the following instances:

I answer the door to find Bobby standing on the steps. He is about nine years old and has frequently been in the house playing with my son. I have often seen him on the street as well. My son has mentioned that Bobby "lives down the street from us" but I don't know where, nor have I ever seen his parents. I ask what he wants and he says, "My mother wants me to ask if I can stay with you while she's in jail." He then goes on to say that she's been "busted." He doesn't say why I've been asked and by now I have come to feel that there is no point inquiring about it.

Keith, whom I have met only casually last summer, comes over around noon. He asks if he can store his banjo with me, and I agree. We take it and put it in the closet, and I anticipate that he will leave. But he seems reluctant to leave, and so I ask him if anything is wrong. He says he wants to talk to me. We go in the kitchen and he begins an elaborate explanation of how he has "messed up his life with crystal" (using methedrine). As he goes on he seems to become more frightened and anxious. Along the way, he says that he has come to my place because everyone else he knows is a "meth freak" and they presumably will be no help. We talk about what he can possibly do. In terms of his present state, the only conceivable immediate action I can see him taking is going to the emergency hospital in the District. I suggest that he think about it; but he decides to call his father in the Midwest instead, and asks if he can use my phone. After he calls his father he says he is much better and is going now. He looks calmer as well. I suggest that he stay here; however, he says he doesn't want to.

He returns about three hours later, in a state of high anxiety again. We sit and talk and pass long periods of silence for almost four hours more. By then I have to leave (both because I have an appointment and because being with Keith for so long has made me tense, anxious, and dreadfully uncertain about what I should do). I suggest that he go to bed, but he says he is too "high" to do that. I then suggest he go stay with some Straight friends of mine, whom he doesn't know but with whom I say he will be comfortable. He agrees (and they do too) so I take him over. Later, the friends I took him to said he stayed until almost midnight, when he said he felt he could "go on."

I have also been requested by members I have just casually known, to store belongings (such as motorcycles or household possessions) which they understood I had room for, and to assist in business dealings with the segments of the Straight community with which they understood I had contact.

Hippies of the Haight may also cope with their troubles by asking members of the Straight community for whatever they need, although by and large this tends to be restricted to asking for money (panhandling) and asking for transportation (hitch-hiking).[5]

More often, members of the Hippie community will co-opt whatever they want from the non-members of the community. "Co-opting" is in essence receiving-without-asking-first. As a sociological form of activity, shoplifting is a substantive example of co-opting: the opportunity to take the merchandise is perceived and acted upon. However, shoplifting is not the only example of coping with one's troubles by co-opting. Taking over vacant houses and apartments in the District for shelter regularly takes place. Similarly, taking over parts of public property (such as parts of the park) occur for the same purpose.[6]

Co-opting from other members of the community may also take place, particularly with respect to shelter. An occasionally mentioned problem that some members face is other members who "request a crash pad for the night and never leave." Those members of the community who have had their shelter so co-opted by others are, of course, put in a difficult position. The moral maxim of sharing plus the obvious fact that they have shelter to spare often results in a situation where the presence of those who stay is tolerated, while complaints are made to others about the co-opters who are unethically "taking advantage" of the situation.

In the same sense, one of the directors of the Happening House, which was established as a locale for various activities of the community, mentioned that eight Hippies "just moved in and stayed one day." He went on to say that when he told them they could not live in the house because "it was for the community as a whole," they responded that "they were in the community." Presumably, this position was ideologically justified because they were there now. Eventually, the director told them that if they did not leave, he would call the police to evict them. As he went on to explain it, "They knew I wouldn't call the police but they also knew I meant what I said about leaving and so they did."

Co-opting involves taking what there is available without asking for it first. It differs from exploitation which involves manipulating the situation in such a way as to create something to take which was not perceivably there before. Exploitation is not a very prevalent means of coping, since the ideological beliefs of the community assume that all there is in the world is given already. This means that the active construction of new possibilities is not a relevant consideration, although it can and does take place with respect to commercial drug transaction. As a matter of my own observations in the community, the only occasions of exploitation I have seen (or heard about from other members) have involved exploitation of monetary situations on the part of sellers of various commodities.

Two examples of such exploitation outside the area of drug transactions are provided by the following field observations:

> I am talking to one of the Hip merchants in his store when an employee from one of the coffee houses comes in to buy something. Ted asks him when the price of coffee (which is now 25¢ a cup) will go down. He says, "When the kids leave for the summer." I presume that the price of coffee went up when the new owner realized that the summer influx would bear it. When I mention this to Ted afterwards, he concurs. (Actually, the price of coffee did not go down until December, since by the end of the summer the regular Hippie population had probably grown accustomed to the higher price.)

> I have just arrived home and am dressed in what are obviously "Straight clothes." I go up to a vendor to buy a copy of one of the Underground newspapers. He says, "25¢." I say, "I thought it was 15¢ in the Bay Area?" He repeats, "It's 25¢." I get the feeling that he thinks it is perfectly acceptable to charge me 25¢ because I look like a tourist who shouldn't really know the price and who shouldn't be given any consideration even if I do. I am tempted to extend the encounter to see what will come of it, but

since I have become a little angry, I decide to drop the matter and buy the paper someplace else.

One would assume that the constructive ideology and logic which is required to embark on an enterprise as a profit-making venture in the first place, is, in effect, all that is necessary to embark on exploiting such situations as well. In this context, common-sense understandings from the conventional world and the Hippie community overlap.

### 3. Explaining

"Coping" involves active manipulation of elements in the members' world as a means of managing their trouble. It rests upon members' perception of alterable elements. But, where members can see no perceivable immediate thing to be done, the form of activity likely to be taken as a strategy for managing their trouble is that of "explanation." "Explanation" as it routinely takes place among the Hippies of the Haight, involves "invoking the bigger picture": perceiving the immediate trouble in terms of its part in some larger event. Within the Hippie community of the Haight, there are two schools of explanation generally sanctioned: the socio-political school, and the mystic school.

The "socio-political" school for the explanation of trouble shares much in common with the explanatory scheme used by the "New Left." There is some overlap between members of the Hippie community and members of the "New Left," and those who are active in both tend routinely to invoke the "socio-political" explanation when explanations are called for. But such explanations are not restricted to this overlapping group. Even Hippies of the Haight who have no involvement in political action at all, and who will insist that "politics is a bad trip," still invoke the "socio-political" school of explanation to account for the presence of "real trouble."

Within the "socio-political" view the trouble any particular member is experiencing is to be understood in terms of the general corruption of the conventional society. Two issues are relevant for the members of the Hippie community invoking this form of explanation. First, the general ideological understanding that the "Establishment" (which refers either to the conventional society in general, or to any particular administrative segment of that society) is not in harmony with nature. Rather, it attempts to superimpose a set of arbitrary criteria on the world as it is given, claiming that that definition, and that definition only, is reality. As it is ideologically given for the members of the Hippie community, there cannot be simply one reality. Any claim made concerning an arbitrarily fixed reality (such as that made by the conventional society) is thus by definition fallacious.

Second, and equally important, the members of the Hippie community derogate the claim of conventional society to, as the Hippies sometimes put it, "have what they think is the final word about reality" as an authoritarian position. For this claim commits members of the conventional society to actions which will enforce that belief about reality—and its concomitant practices—on others.

In effect, within the socio-political explanatory system, the conventional society is determined to superimpose an untenable system of life upon the world. And such a misguided enterprise on the part of the conventional society can only result in trouble, particularly for those who desire to be free.

The socio-political explanation for trouble is most frequently invoked when trouble for members is widespread in the community, as when members of the conventional society define such Hippie activities as happenings in the park as "civic disturbances" and take police action to curb them.

In the same sense, however, when the members of the conventional society refuse to acknowledge and assist in what members of the Hippie community consider "reasonable" solutions to problems, the refusal is understood by the Hippies to rest upon the conventional society's fear of acknowledging an alternative way of life. The following field observations provide three examples of the sense in which the socio-political explanation is used to explain general problems in the Hippie community. The first example comes from a Town Hall Meeting (a rather short-lived attempt to provide a common meeting ground for both the Straight and Hippie residents of the Haight). The other two come from informal conversations between Hippies:

> The potential problems which an influx of young people into the District this summer (1967) may pose, have been raised by one of the Hippies in the audience, who states that "we (in an undifferentiated sense) will have to do something about it." In the course of the general discussion, one of the Hippies suggests setting up a large tent in Golden Gate Park, to house the new arrivals. A number of the Straights assert that they do not see why they should be responsible for the care and well-being of what they consider to be "outsiders." Two or three Straight speakers are adamant that what should "be done by the District" is to inform those young people who are planning to come in the summer that there are no facilities for them and hence they should not come. One Straight speaker says "we (again, undifferentiated) should tell them to stay away, that they're not welcome here."
>
> The counterargument presented by the Hippies is that the young people should be free to do what they want to do. And if what they want to do is come to the Haight this summer, those who are here not only have the obligation to accept the arrival of newcomers, but a duty to help them in their life in the District by providing at least shelter.
>
> One of the Hippies gets up and argues that the Straights who say there is no room for the newcomers do not even know what they are talking about. He goes on at length saying that there are large numbers of churches in the District which could house many people when church services and activities are not in progress. He continues by saying, essentially to the Straights, "They (the churches) don't *have* to be locked up and empty at night. You just think they do, and you're wrong."
>
> The topic of discussion has been a number of narcotic raids made in the District in the past few weeks. None of the speakers have been personally involved, nor do they know anyone who has. What seems to be of general concern, however, is that the raids have taken place at all. Janet says, "They're (the conven-

tional society) so afraid of drugs because they know that if they (drugs) are used, everyone will see how phoney America really is."

Paul has been "rapping" about how corrupt the conventional society is. He goes on to say that the Hippies' dropping out frightens the members of the conventional society because it suggests to the latter that there is another way of life. "They can't take that, you know. They have to have the only way of life—their thing for everybody, whether they want it or not."

Somewhat later in the conversation, someone says that the landlords in the Haight "have been refusing to rent to Hippies because they think they (the Hippies) will bring their property values down. That's all they think about. Money and property values and more money."

But the socio-political explanation may also be brought in by individual members as a reasonable account for their individual problems. Any trouble in the maintenance of one's body, such as trouble in obtaining food, shelter, or money, may be thus explained in terms of being "the way America is."

Excerpts from members' conversations provide three illustrations:

Craig has been looking for a job for the past two days. He says he "knows a lot" about electronics, but the companies at which he applied have turned him down. Perry responds to Craig's remarks by saying, in a mocking tone: "You have long hair and wear a beard. How can you know anything about electronics?" The implication of Perry's response is that this is what Craig's prospective employers thought about him and this is why they did not hire him.

Carla has been working in an office downtown for the past three days. She says, "I have to dress so Straight every day. It really brings me down. I wish I could find a job where I could be myself." Ruth laughs and says, "All the Straights are schizophrenic, so if you want to work for Straights, you have to be schizophrenic, too."

William is rapping about the war. He says, "America only thinks the world is free if they're controlling it." He goes on to say that if America were a really "moral" country, it would be feeding the people of Asia, instead of fighting them. Someone in the group says that America should be feeding the Hippies in the Haight who don't have food, too. Ernest then remarks, "That's their (the conventional society's) thing—to make war. I just wish that they would leave me alone." (Ernest has recently had to or three altercations with the police on the street. These have involved being detained and questioned, although not arrested.)

The members of the Hippie community may also employ a socio-political explanation for the troublesome behavior of other members of the community. The general form, as illustrated by the following field observation, is to account for another member's activity in terms of his being "on a power trip."

George has just left the apartment. While he was there Frank had been trying to fix his record player and George kept telling Frank that he didn't know what he was doing. Frank became visibly angry, although the other three seemed to ignore the interaction between him and George. After George has left, Janet says to Frank: "Why do you let George get you uptight? He's on a power trip, so just forget about him."

To be on a "power trip" is to be actively attempting to impose one's will, aims, goals, or desires on another. Thus, to describe another member as being "on a power trip" is to assert that he can only see *one* reality in the given situation. However, the implication of the phrase, as it is used by members of the Hippie community about other members, is that members who are "on a power trip" are not necessarily committed to that position. Rather, what is implied is that eventually, because the other *is* a Hippie (and hence has either had the vision or is capable of having it in the future) his troublesome behavior is only temporary.

Thus, while within the framework of the socio-political explanation members will describe other members who attempt to dominate or control a situation as "being on a power trip," for Straights who engage in the same kind of behavior, the phrase which is used is "power is their thing." Presumably, the understanding is that domination and control for the latter is what they *want* to do, while domination and control on the part of the former is what they may *happen* to be doing at the present moment.

From my observations, the "socio-political" school of explanation has been present as a sanctioned means of explaining trouble in the Haight from the beginning of the community. The "mystic" school seems to have come into general prevalence much later.

"Mysticism" is distinguished in the Hippie community from "Eastern Philosophy." Eastern philosophy, particularly Zen Buddhism, like the "socio-political" school of explanation, apparently was integral in the foundation and organization of the basic ideology of the Hippie community; it thus serves as a basic ontological system.

But "mysticism" (which includes both Eastern and Western mysticism) can be characterized as an epistemological system, related to the general philosophical foundation of the Hippie ideology. It is related in the same way that "science" is related to the general Western philosophical foundation of the ideology in the conventional community. For example, where a member of the conventional community might explain the falling of an apple from a tree by invoking the Newtonian law of gravity, a member of the Hippie community might explain the same event by invoking the "Karma" of the apple—its intrinsic fate is eventually to fall from the tree.

The most prevalent mystic practices in the community are astrology, the I-Ching, and the Tarot cards. These tend to be the most highly explicated systems of explanation, although in addition, Karma (as fate or destiny) and "vibrations" (as intuition) may be also used to explain whatever is seen by members as requiring explanation.

These last two, "Karma" and "vibrations," tend to be used in the same way that members of the conventional community use explanations such as "God's will" and "human nature." The following field observations provide three examples of how "Karma" and "vibrations" are invoked as general explanations for, in these cases, "general troubles." [7]

Four of us are on our way to the beach. There has not been much talking in the car at all. Suddenly Frances says (apropos of nothing that I can see), "The reason children and their parents have so much conflict is that you are born into families who can teach you what you still have to learn (as a part of your Karma) and that's always hard in the beginning."

Two people are talking, sitting in the park. The gist of their conversation is that the scene on Haight Street has "begun to deteriorate" and the "reason" given to account for this deterioration is "bad vibrations" (presumably emanating from outside the District, but this is not stated explicitly).

Janet and someone I have not met before are discussing a mutual acquaintance. The specific topic of their discussion is that fact that he has been "busted" for possession of drugs again. Both of them acknowledge that the bust (which seems to be the third one he has encountered) is a "bad scene." The male concludes the conversation by saying, in a somewhat remorseful tone of voice: "Man, that's his Karma."

Similarly, occasions when diffuse trouble has taken place on the street evoke members' comments on the presence of "bad vibrations." And so, for example, any time the conventional community defines the action of the street as a "civic disturbance" or "riot," and the police are called in, the consequences are "diffuse trouble," which is described as "bad vibrations."

In contrast to "Karma" and "vibrations," astrology, the I-Ching, and the Tarot Cards tend to be employed as much more systematic formulations of explanation. These formulations subsume the reason for the particular trouble under a more general theory for why the world is as it is. Since particular troubles for members tend to be individual troubles (troubles encountered by individual members), these systematic mystical explanations serve the purpose of putting the trouble into its proper perspective by making the trouble no longer a unique, randomly fortuitous event. Instead it becomes an instance of "troubles" that could have been encountered by anyone who had been in the individual's particular situation at that time.

The following excerpts from field observations provide one example of the process:

> Peter and Nora are talking about Peter's general psychic state of the past few weeks. Peter says, "I've been down (depressed). I don't know why. Nothing particular has happened." Nora responds, "Your planets are in retrograde. It's been that way for three weeks. There's nothing you can do about it." Nora goes on to explain that because of the "retrograde motion of the planets," things have been "generally bad for everybody." Since the topic of Peter's depression is dropped after this, it seems that the explanation has been adequate.

The ideological tenets of the community place emphasis on the individual members as persons special and unique in themselves. These tenets of the community also postulate a universal community of mankind. But not infrequently, the special and unique attributes of the individual members are not in accordance with the understanding of a compatible universe of mankind. In other words, members are not always in agreement about some particular aspect of their world. Yet their ideology would lead them to expect that they would be. At the same time, the ideology provides good reasons for each to maintain his original position. In effect, the belief in the compatible collectivity of mankind and the value of individual uniqueness may generate a particular set of difficult conditions. Under these conditions, amelioration of incompatible differences between members by any kind of change or compromise on the part of the members makes no sense. Of course, as already suggested (when discussing the maintenance of one's psyche), members have the sanctioned option of simply "quitting the scene" when they feel uncomfortable in the situation. But other options are also possible.

In such cases of incompatible differences, if individuals do not wish to avoid "trouble" by avoiding the situation in which personal differences may generate "trouble," such "trouble" may then be managed, not by ameliorative practices, but by explanatory practices. Thus, the "trouble" still exists, but it makes sense that it should exist as it does.

Astrological theory, which incorporates within it the concept of "incompatible" signs, thus provides a comprehensible means both to explain personal differences and to permit the situation to continue as one of the facts of life which must be accepted in the world as given. The following field example is typical of the kinds of situations in which the astrological signs of the members are treated as relevant matters:

> Roy makes a very dogmatic statement about what the "Straight society" is all about. I sigh audibly to express my annoyance with him. He responds, "I am a Libra."
>
> Out of curiosity, I respond, "I'm a Pisces," and he says, "I have some friends who are Pisces." The implication of this last interchange seems to be that our rather precarious relationship can be explained in terms of the incompatibility of Libra and Pisces.
>
> However, I later ask someone else about it and he tells me that Libra and Pisces are actually more or less neutral, and that we should have found out what signs each of us had rising since our incompatibility may have been generated more by our "rising" signs than by our "natal" signs.

Even when there are no perceivable difficulties between members, the astrological signs of the participants may be brought in as a way of accounting for whatever is present in the situation, whether problematic or not.[8] Field observations provide an example of such general explanatory activity:

> I am talking with Harry, whom I've just met. We are talking about astrology in general, and various unrelated matters such as dogs, school, and people we mutually know. Suddenly, in the course of the conversation, Marilyn says, "You're a Sagittarius." I reply, "No, I'm a Pisces." However, Harry, who has drawn my natal horoscope (but not interpreted it for me), says, "You have Sagittarius rising."
>
> Although at this time the meaning of Marilyn's remark escapes me, Harry produces a smile of vindication showing that we are

both right. I later learn that one's basic personality is to be explained in terms of both one's natal sign and one's rising sign, as well. Finally, for full specification, one's Moon sign and the distribution of one's planets at the time of birth must be taken into consideration.

In the conventional world of middle-class American life, such a "general understanding" of the other person may be developed by invoking his political affiliations, religious affiliation, or social class background. Thus, within the conventional world, I have heard one member explain why another member is as he is by saying, "He is a John Bircher," "He is a Catholic," "That's his Puritan background," and "He grew up in a working-class environment." [9]

Insofar as the mystical systems are general theories, they may be employed not only for "putting real trouble" into perspective, but also as a rational ground for preventive practices. In my observations of the Hippies of the Haight, the I-Ching and the Tarot were frequently used as systems which could produce preventive measures. But these systems require considerable technical understanding. For example, there are Hippies of the Haight who believe in astrology as a valid epistemological system, yet I have never seen or heard them mention using the daily horoscope forecast (found in the major newspapers and also in numerous astrology magazines available at almost any newsstand in the city), as a form of preventive practice. When I have asked why this is the case, two reasons have generally been given. First, the understanding of those who acknowledge astrology as a valid epistemological system places emphasis on more than just the "natal" sign. In order to employ astrology properly for fully understanding and hence successfully predicting outcomes, one must consider at least the rising sign of the subject in question as well. His Moon sign, and the particular distribution and relationship of his planets at time and place of birth are also understood to be integral matters for accurate prediction. To interpret the forthcoming day on the basis of natal sign alone (as it appears in both the newspaper horoscope and the astrology magazines) is to simplify the matter to the point of likely distortion of the "facts."

The world as it is given is an infinitely complex phenomenon where "reality" can be distorted by facile generalizations in the general understanding of the members of the Hippie community. For the Hippies committed to astrology, this general understanding of the world, along with their rather extensive knowledge about astrology, results in a situation where what they consider to be "mass-produced natal forecasts" are meaningless or irrelevant to their lives.

The second reason which Hippies may give for why astrology is not used for preventive practices is that technique, judgment, and intuition are all required. The casting of a full natal horoscope is simply a matter of technique, something which can be done by anyone who knows the date, time, and place of birth of an individual, and has the proper reference books. And Hippies refer to those who do draw up such horoscopes as "technical astrologers." The interpretation of such charts, however, is another matter. Or more specifically, it is two other matters. Although not all "technical astrologers" in the community provide even general interpretations of the charts they draw, many do. However, the general understanding of astrology among the Hippies of the Haight includes within it the general interpretation of planetary relationships. This general interpretation is a matter of personality and characterological traits which are associated with such things as the position of particular planets and the relationship between planets.

At the time of a person's birth, the particular planetary constellations which exist and can be seen from the "perspective" of his birthplace (where he's at when he's born) are the basic influences on his personality and character. In a manner of speaking, like the conventional understanding of the effect of heredity and environment, what a person will ultimately be is determined by where and when he is born. Hence, natal horoscopes are analogous to psychological tests: they reveal the general personality traits and characterological dispositions of the subject, but do not specify any particular course of action he will undertake in any specific situation.

Specific forecasts can be made on the basis of one's complete natal horoscope and knowledge of "situational conditions." [10] But such specific forecasts (such as what will happen on the ensuing day, week, or month), require not only an extensive knowledge of the astrological features of the world, but special psychic abilities in order to be able to properly employ this knowledge as a means of "reading the future." For most Hippies, extensive knowledge of the world is irrelevant; and for astrologically committed Hippies, such psychic abilities are considered not only special, but relatively rare. Therefore, even though it is understood that it is possible to predict ensuing events on the basis of astrology, there are few opportunities to have this prediction made.

These difficulties do not present themselves to members using either the I-Ching or the Tarot. Where astrology is treated as a "conditional" epistemological system, the I-Ching and the Tarot are treated as "determinate" epistemological systems. As members have explained it on a number of occasions, "all the knowledge of the universe is contained within the I-Ching and/or the Tarot cards." Since in this sense "it is all there," it is in effect easier to read the I-Ching or the Tarot cards as predictions of ensuing events in store for the subject than it is to use astrology.[11]

Thus, "casting a Hexagram and reading the I-Ching" and "dealing the cards and reading the Tarot" constitute sanctionable preventive practices as well as a means of explanation.

Hippies of the Haight who employ mysticism for preventive practices may do so ritually or only occasionally. I have met some (and also heard about other members of the community) who begin their day by "casting the I-Ching." In contrast, the reading of the Tarot cards tends to be only occasionally employed as a preventive practice. However, in both (as the field observations below illustrate), if a reading of either is made, it is understood to reveal "true" predictions of what will ensue for the subject.

Five acquaintances are talking about going to the country for the week. Someone had proposed it earlier, and it seemed to be generally understood that all of them would go. The matter has come up now as a topic for speculation. However, Myron now says he will not go to the country with the rest of the group. He says he has cast the I-Ching and the answer is no. Everybody seems to accept it as a reasonable and sufficient explanation for his change of mind (as though among members of the conventional community he had said, "I have to work.")

The following was observed among a group of five or six people lolling on Haight Street: the general topic of their conversation was the various geographical locations of the Hippie community. One of the participants remarks, "I am going to Arizona. I cast my I-Ching and it said to seek out friends in the Southwest."

Nora, Carol, and I go to Eric's apartment. Nora has called a few minutes before, asking if Eric would do a "30-day reading" (of the cards, in this case regular playing cards) for us. Eric reads my cards first, then Nora's. For Nora he reads that there "will be a substantial amount of money coming from a man." Nora says she doubts it; she doesn't know anyone with any substantial amount of money, particularly one who would give it to her. Then she says, somewhat abstractly, "Well, maybe Roy's (her husband) grandfather."

For Carol, Eric provides the following "prediction": "A man you know will ask you to go on a long trip with him, but it will turn out badly—emotionally and physically." Carol looks worried (almost frightened) and says, "Duane (a fellow she has known more or less casually) has asked me to go down the coast with him." She goes on to say that she was planning to go, but now she will not.

On the way back to Nora's apartment, Carol continues to talk about Eric's reading, essentially concluding that it was fortunate that we had gone to Eric's since otherwise she might have gone with Duane (and, presumably, experienced the misfortunes Eric "foresaw").

Similarly, the ineffable notion of "vibrations" may be employed as a method of preventive practices. The "receipt" of "bad vibrations" from either another person or from the situation in

general may be provided as reasonable grounds for specific formulations of plans for subsequent action. From my observations of
the invocation of "bad vibrations" they tend to be used in a casual
and somewhat all-purpose way. Once one has decided that some
particular person has "bad vibrations for me" or some particular
scene "is full of bad vibrations," it makes rational sense for one,
and others as well, to avoid such persons or places in the future
and so to avoid encountering "real trouble."

The I-Ching and the Tarot may be read without being employed as preventive practices. That is, they may be read without
the subject formulating his plans of action for the ensuing days in
terms of what was read. In such cases, the I-Ching and the Tarot
readings are used as post-hoc explanations for whatever may be
encountered in the course of the ensuing days.

> Dorothy mentions to me that she "cast the I-Ching this morn-
> ing and I knew it was going to be a bad day." This she said after
> recounting an unpleasant incident with a co-worker.

> Three of us are talking in the kitchen. Nora mentions, some-
> what casually, that she had the cards read for her and they
> forecast that she would take a trip. She then went on to explain
> that she did in fact go to the country, although it was "unex-
> pected" when it happened (i.e., she had not really planned on
> going, but it was something that came up suddenly with another
> group of people).

> David is telling me of an unpleasant disturbance that he wit-
> nessed. Included in his account of the events is the remark that
> an acquaintance of his told him, as the two of them were
> witnessing the scene: "I cast the I-Ching this morning and it
> said, 'there will be conflict.'" (David is annoyed because he feels
> his friend was pleased with the disturbance since it provided him
> with evidence of the validity of the reading.)

The above example suggests a more general point—that
epistemological systems can be at variance with one another within the general belief system employed in the Hippie community.
Mysticism as either a preventive practice or an explanatory system
is not uniformly accepted within the Hippie community as a sanc-

tioned activity. A similar example is contained in the following excerpts from field observations:

> Owen is recounting an "unpleasant" evening he had just had. It involved some girl he was with who, he explained, "was on some mystic trip. That was all she would talk about." This, Owen explained, "got on his nerves." He said he finally walked out and left her in the doughnut shop.

Similarly, a number of Hippies in the Haight have essentially said, "I don't understand the mysticism thing," and presumably, what is implied in their "not understanding" it is "not accepting" it either. As mentioned previously, this position tends to be taken most adamantly by those who employ the "socio-political" scheme of explanation of the world, but it is not unique to them. Some who consistently employ no particular explanatory scheme have mentioned it also.

To my knowledge, other mystical systems for explanation (such as palmistry and graphology) are not utilized by the Hippies of the Haight, even though they are easily accessible as systems employed by some segments of the conventional society. Numerology, which is occasionally considered within the I-Ching and within the Tarot, does not seem to enter in the ideology of the Hippie community in any extensive way either, although I have encountered two or three members who have asserted that they "have an interest in numerology."

Explanatory systems which are not unique to the Hippie community itself are often employed by the members of the community. What for all practical purposes looks just like "Conventional Individual Psychology" and "Conventional Commonsense" are perhaps as generally prevalent as the "socio-political" school and the "mystic school." This overlapping with conventional belief systems is often found in that segment of the Hippie community which can be defined as "the self-seekers." Within the segment, "finding oneself" constitutes the basic task at hand and the principles for undertaking it are essentially introspective consideration of one's motives for acting and one's habits of reacting to the actions of others. Although they do not necessarily invoke the name of the conventional authorities in individual psychology (and while they occasionally base their undertaking on Eastern systems such as Yoga) the principles they formulate appear to be the same as those of "Conventional Individual Psychology."

Similarly, what appears to be "Conventional Commonsense" can be seen by the judgments made by the members of the Hippie community. However the use here (as in the conventional community) is eminently casual—it is treated as matters that any normal person could be expected to know already. The following field observation provides one example:

> I have picked up a hitchhiker. He is on his way to the beach in Marin County. On the drive he explains that he has been living with friends in the Haight after he left the place he was staying in Marin. In response to my question of why he left Marin, he explains that the Hippies who stay there would "steal" his jewelry-making materials. I go on to say that I thought that never happened, that Hippies never stole from other Hippies. His response is, "There are bad Hippies just as there are bad Straights. But there are less bad Hippies than there are bad ones in other scenes." Presumably, the import of his last statement is that no one can expect perfection on the part of all the members of the community, although by definition, being a Hippie is likely to bring one closer to community-sanctioned ideals than membership in any other group would.

In the same sense, both dealers and buyers may invoke a kind of "conventional human nature" explanation for why commercial transactions of drugs in the Hippie community exist as they do in the first place. But they also invoke explanations based on the socio-political school (such as the influence of the capitalist system) or explanations based on the mystic school (such as the influence of the planetary system).

Preventive practices, methods of coping, and the system of explanation which result from the particular beliefs which the Hippies of the Haight hold about the world are meaningful and appropriate. The community sanction of such procedures is based

on what members of the group know already concerning the world
—the knowledge they do not doubt to be true or think insignificant.
In effect, this system of beliefs provides a specification of just
what matters are to be given consideration in the management of
one's troubles and the reasons why such matters are relevant in
the present situation.

Thus, the systems of explanation provided by the socio-political school and the mystical school both fit within the framework of
interpretation of the ideological tenets. The former stresses that
the conventional community is not in harmony with nature; the
latter, that the Hippies are in harmony with visions. Thus, there is
no greater general ideological sanction for one as a system of
explanation than there is for the other. And so, as a matter of
practical choice for members, one practice is ideologically as
adequate as the other when events turn out differently from what
members reasonably had expected.

Similarly, in "buying grass" when a member can reasonably
expect a transaction of "good prospects," but that transaction turns
out to be "a burn," he has a variety of means to account for the
perceived discrepancy. He may first review the various components
of his actual practices to see whether in fact they were the same as
the sanctioned components.[12] But, if he is satisfied that his practices were the same as sanctioned practices, this discrepancy is in
no way obvious evidence discounting his ideological assumptions
about the world. Now he may turn to further specification or
explanation.

Those who employ the socio-political school of explanation
may invoke the bigger picture by showing the influence of the capitalistic system on the bad transaction; while those who employ the
mystic school may invoke the bigger picture by showing the influence of the planetary system on it. The practice of "burning" people who buy grass is not a sanctioned practice in the community.
But neither is it a contingency outside the realm of ideologically
comprehensible considerations.

In effect, such systems of explanations differ only in the particular ideological stress they embody. Either provides a meaningful way to continue the basic ideological tenets they support, and hence in turn sustain those beliefs even in the face of *any given instance of failure.*[13] In this sense, any personal trouble can be structured in terms of an ideological framework of interpretation. The framework suggests what to take into consideration, how these matters should be considered; and what kinds of explanations may be offered to account for personal troubles. In this way, *personal* problems are provided with their *social* meaning.

## NOTES

1. This same kind of decision can also be found among Orthodox Jews who refuse to eat in restaurants which are not completely Kosher. See, for example, Howard Polsky, "A Study of Orthodoxy in Milwaukee," in M. Sklare, ed., *The Jews* (Glencoe, Ill.: The Free Press, 1958), pp. 325–335.

2. The use of other occult systems for preventive practices will be discussed in the section on "explaining."

3. Relevant here is Morris Opler, "Themes as Dynamic Forces in Culture," *AJS,* Vol. 51 (1946), pp. 198–206. Opler focuses on culture themes (as members' beliefs about what "should" take place in their world) as *limiting factors* for members' behavior. A substantive example can be found in Frederick Fliegel and Joseph Kivlin, "Attributes of Innovations as Factors in Diffusion," *AJS,* Vol. 72 (1966), pp. 235–248.

4. Hippies may also make requests for cigarettes, matches, directions, and other kinds of information, just as requests may be made in the conventional community. Parenthetically, food as well as the apocryphal "flowers" are often simply given to others on the street without any request on the part of the receiver. Similarly, at least among friends, beads and various trip-toys may also be spontaneously given.

5. On one occasion, when there was a disturbance on the street (ostensibly caused by some Black adolescents breaking one of the store windows) there were a number of Hippies milling around asking one another where the police were (before the latter arrived). Similarly, when the Free Medical Clinic first closed for lack of funds,

conversations among some members implied that the city could well afford to subsidize the clinic, and therefore should. However, requests for general assistance from the conventional community tend to be rare.

6. The "normal trouble" of just having a place to be while one is just being may involve co-opting activities such as using cars parked along the street and doorsteps for benches. In the spring and early part of the summer of 1967, the doorsteps facing onto Haight Street were co-opted as stalls for Hippies peddling jewelry, or work, and sometimes food. As I learned from my son, the peddlers who so co-opted the doorsteps used them as fixed addresses. I further found out, in looking for my son one afternoon (after he simply said he would be "with his friend who sold God's Eyes on the doorsteps") that which doorstep was "the God's Eyes peddlers' doorstep" was common knowledge among those peddling other varieties of merchandise from the doorsteps.

7. In this sense, "bad vibrations" for the Hippies of the Haight play a role in their everyday life which is formally analogous to the role played by "ghosts" for the Ifaluk of Micronesia. Cf. Melford Spiro, "Ghosts, Ifaluk and Teleological Functionalism," *American Anthropology,* Vol. 54 (1952), pp. 497–503. A similar situation is found for the Navaho of the southwest. See, Claude Kluckhohn, *Navaho Witchcraft,* papers for the Peabody Museum, XXLL, No. 2, 1944.

8. From observations made in working class neighborhoods and in mystic bookshops in the conventional community, it appears that the members of the conventional community who believe in astrology use it both for accounting for difficulties and for making sense of non-problematic situations as well.

9. Such accounts for "understanding the other" may also be invoked by the individual they refer to as a means of his explaining himself to the others.

10. Here, predicting by means of astrology is formally the same as predicting by means of science. One's horoscope stands as "general laws" about the person, which, taken in conjunction with a set of specifiable conditions, permit specific predictions of outcomes. For the general logic underlying such predictions, see R. B. Braithwaite, *Scientific Explanation* (New York: Harper Torchbooks, 1963), pp. 22–49. Bronislaw Malinowski argues that the distinction between magic (and mysticism in general) and science can be maintained by virtue of whether the explanatory system in question is based on

general or specific experience, reasonableness of predicted outcome or mere hope; logic or desire; or whether it refers to the profane or the sacred orders of everyday life. See *Magic, Science and Religion* (Garden City, N.Y.: Doubleday Anchor Books, 1948), especially pp. 85–87. However, in terms of members' practical employment of such systems of explanation in everyday life, Malinowski's conceptual distinction is difficult to maintain. When the scientific and mystic beliefs held by members are taken in conjunction with their everyday practical activities, a more adequate conceptualization seems to be that both science and mysticism provide quite encompassing systems of explanation. For a fuller discussion of this position, see E. E. Evans Pritchard, *Witchcraft, Oracles and Magic Among the Azande* (Oxford: Oxford University Press), as well as Michael Polyani, *Personal Knowledge* (New York: Harper Torchbooks, 1964), particularly pages 287–298.

11. In astrology, the I-Ching, and the Tarot, the "bits of information" they produce are read in terms of a given array of relationships between the units used to get the information. In astrology, these bits of information are the signs of the zodiac, the houses, and the planets; in the I-Ching, these bits are the 64 hexagrams; and in the Tarot they are the 22 major arcana cards and the 56 cards of the minor arcana. Thus, taken by themselves, the I-Ching and the Tarot can provide more bits of information insofar as they contain a greater number of different possibilities.

12. Cf. Malinowski, *op. cit.*

13. Repeated failure is not the issue here, but *any given instance* of failure which a member may encounter at *any given time*.

# Part Four

# CONCLUSIONS

# 9

## Everyday Life in the Haight

The tenets of the Hippie ideology propose for members a set of assumptions about the world—assumptions that, when *proclaimed in general*, appear unified and consistent. For those who accept it, the ideology is understood as constituting the fundamental truth concerning the world, and hence, as providing the basic moral imperatives by which each member is to conduct his affairs and judge the affairs of others. However, the ideology as proclaimed by members is not a logical argument in and of itself. Rather, it provides the premises from which logical arguments on the part of members are to proceed.[1] As Egon Bittner has suggested,[2]

> The objects and events that an ordinary person encounters, recognizes, judges and acts upon in the course of his everyday life do not have unequivocally stable meanings. This is not to say that recognition, judgment and action are not normatively governed, but that the ordinarily competent person *is required* to use practical wisdom to interpret the relevance of a rule to a particular instance of the typified situation to which the rule presumably pertains.

Thus, to become a "competent Hippie" requires more than simply learning the ideology as a catechism. It requires, as well, learning how to interpret those catechistic principles as an accounting scheme for matters relevant to practical action.[3]

Once a commitment to the ideology has been made by flesh and blood people, living their everyday lives in accordance with the tenets of that ideology is managed by members as they individually perceive the ideologically-relevant aspects of the everyday situations they encounter. They make judgments and decisions they consider "reasonable" on ideologically warranted grounds, and they expect that other members, collectively knowing what each member knows individually, will understand the meaning of these judgments and concur. In this way, the ideological beliefs of a group provide the meaning of life for members individually, and at the same time, establish the boundaries for the set of sanctioned practices that will be recognized by the group collectively.[4]

In no sense do the Hippies of the Haight *enact* their beliefs as such on a day-to-day basis. However, in a variety of ways they *act with respect* to those beliefs, treating the beliefs as warrantable premises concerning the world—as matters not to be doubted in subsequent deliberations. The beliefs of individual members provide the import and signification of the actual circumstances of their lives. By codifying the subsequent content of members' perceived reality, their beliefs may be thought of as giving the terms by which their everyday lives will be defined.

In so defining the terms for individual members, the ideological tenets held by members collectively establish the sanctionable boundaries for their collective practices. What is held as matters of common knowledge for members—what any normal member can be expected to know—are what will be considered the warrantable grounds for social action. Such matters, in being shared in common by members, are subsequently treated by them as "self-evident truths."[5]

Such "self-evident truths" define what universe of social things exists as given; and ultimately they characterize each given social thing as one which is to be sanctioned or censured by group members. As matters *already* interpreted, the ideological beliefs of a group are analogous to a childhood primer, in which the things of the world are named and the words "good," "bad," and "neutral," presented in conjunction with the name. The analogy, however, is at best a vague connotation of the *way* the ideological beliefs of the group establish the sanctionable boundaries for members' practices.

For every society, regardless of its specific circumstances, there are very general courses of action members can undertake during the ongoing course of the day. Members must decide upon what particular practices to engage in, in some sensible and sanctioned way. Members must be able to evaluate their circumstances as information relevant to subsequent action. Members must be able to manage whatever goods, commodities, or services they deem relevant. All of these general courses of action, and others, are individual problems at one level. That is, they are problems that each individual member of a group is likely to face as he lives out his individual life.

However, rarely if ever, can individual members point to any explicit formulation (any such existing primer) of the innumerable sanctioned and censured practices they both recognize and expect to have recognized by other competent members of the community. Yet members routinely make such judgments and make them with a sense of assurance that other competent members of the community would make similar judgments.[6]

Furthermore, when called upon, individual members characteristically justify the sanctioned properties of their actions and judgments by invoking the ideological principles they claim members believe. By and large, the belief system so invoked does not resemble an explicit codification of the members' judgmental activity. The ideological beliefs of any given member may be self-consciously held, but they are rarely explicitly held; nor is their interrelationship often a matter of Talmudic debate. In some areas, or perhaps for some members, segments of that belief system may be articulated so that their consistency and inter-related character is also made clear. For example, the moral precepts can be related to one another in this way. But ordinarily, the explicit invocation of *some* segment of those beliefs will serve as adequate justification for action when justification is called for.

At most then, the ideological beliefs function *for the members* as an idealized version of their understanding of the world. Members do not treat the ideology as a literal description of their world, but address it as a set of true assumptions which they hold concerning the-world-in-general. Thus, if members are to act with proper consideration for the specifics of the present situation, they must interpret the specific meanings of their actual circumstances in terms of the relevant beliefs that compose that idealized *Weltanschauung*.

For the Hippies of the Haight, considerations which their ideology makes relevant are found in the practical activity of living out typical days. The Hippies of the Haight order their day (and in more general terms, their lives) by evaluating the present moment in a particular way—in terms of whether their circumstances are in accord with the ideologically justified features of the world they anticipate. As matters of practical action, the daily round constitutes possible activities that may be engaged in or not, according to the personal mood of individual members. Furthermore, the sanctioned structure of those activities is one which maximizes individual pleasure and satisfaction. And this focus develops for both individual activities (such as dressing, eating, and just being) and also for collective activities (such as being social and happenings). The maximization of individual satisfactions is part of collective action since the sanctioned structure of collective activities is one of simultaneity rather than sequence of action.

The kinds of consideration the ideology of the Hippies of the Haight makes relevant are also found in the ways members assess their present situation. The ideologically relevant question for the members is not one which addresses the *status of the action*, but the *status of the experience*. In this sense, the sanctioned terms of such evaluations are not formulated in terms of standards of performance (e.g., "right" or "wrong"), but in terms of practical standards of experience (e.g., "groovy" or "a hassle").

Thus for the Hippies of the Haight, things do not so much "go wrong" for them as they "turn out different" from expectations predicted on the basis of their beliefs. The kinds of trouble they perceive as real trouble are in areas of ideologically relevant activities. Thus, "not getting ahead" in one's job is not trouble; but "not being free" in one's job is. In this sense, the full meaning of the experience of either normal or real trouble in those ideologically relevant areas rests on the collective definition of the situation. It rests, that is, on the ideological understanding by members of the significance of any problem and their practical understanding of the ideologically justified features of their daily round. In this way, the meaning of present experience serves to establish the conditions of subsequent action; for once the nature of the situation can be assessed, rational courses of action can be formulated. The rationality of such courses of action is not found in the particular practice undertaken, but in the members' perceived appropriateness of the practice in relation to their assessment of the situation. Just as it is in the conventional society, one form of "irrationality" for the Hippies of the Haight is "making a mountain out of a molehill." Thus, among the Hippies of the Haight, one does not attempt actively to manage one's situation unless that situation warrants management in ideological terms. Yet once the situation is properly defined as consequential, there are a variety of sanctioned choices available to members as reasonable plans for managing their trouble.

The routine ways of managing trouble and the routine ways of obtaining goods have been considered in terms of sanctioned options which members may select as they perceive the warrant for them. Like the practices which constitute the round of every-

day activity, the practices which the Hippies of the Haight employ
as means of managing trouble and obtaining goods are structured
in terms of the beliefs they hold about their world. In this sense,
what kinds of activities will be sanctioned (for example as
"preventive practices") are defined in terms of members' understandings about the body and the psyche; their understanding
about the drug experience; and their understanding about the
universe-in-general. Similarly, what kinds of activities will be
sanctioned as methods of coping, or what systems of explanations
are acceptable, will be defined in terms of members' understanding of their world. This understanding will encompass what parts
of their world are fixed elements and what parts of their world
are variable; what the possibilities are for active manipulation by
members; and what external elements are likely to influence their
situation. As beliefs, these matters are treated as "self-evident
truths," what everyone around here knows as common knowledge.[7] Yet, at the same time, social action is, in Weber's terms,
guided in its course by the meaning which the actors subjectively
hold. Thus, considerations of coping by asking or coping by co-
opting, considerations of explaining in terms of the influence of
the capitalistic or the planetary system are all justified by the
members' ideological understanding of "what the world is like"
and "what is likely in the world."

Thus, if members assume, as their first order of business, that
the beliefs they hold about their world are warrantable matters
for themselves and others as well, and if they assume further that
those beliefs are to be guiding principles for their conduct, then
"commonsense" must be brought into play, whereby the ideology
is addressed as a method of giving due consideration to matters
of experiential knowledge of the past, matters of reasonable conjecture concerning the future, matters of likely purpose and in-
tention, and matters of possible contingencies.[8] In this way, individual members subscribing to some given set of beliefs can
independently come to similar decisions in the appropriate cir-

cumstances; and they subsequently produce those regular and routine patterns of social action which characterize the collective group life.

## NOTES

1. The "straight line" model does not fit the program of "servomechanisms" which address self-correcting machines whose corrective program supplements its primary function program. Cf. George Miller, Eugene Galanter, and Karl Pribram, *Plans and the Structure of Behavior* (New York: Holt, Rinehart, and Winston, 1960), pp. 31–44, and Walter Buckley, *Sociology and Modern Systems Theory* (Englewood Cliffs, N.J.: Prentice-Hall, 1967), pp. 42–81.

2. "Radicalism and Radical Movements," *American Sociological Review*, Vol. 28 (1963), p. 930, emphasis in the original. For a general discussion of the role of members' logic in the maintenance of the stability of group life, see Godfry and Monica Wilson, *The Analysis of Social Change* (Cambridge: Cambridge University Press, 1954), pp. 53–56. Of particular importance with respect to the present study is the Wilsons' analysis of logic as a procedure for the sanctioned qualification of members' assertions about the state of affairs their world contains. The same general point is employed by L. Thompson, "Logico-Aesthetic Integration of Hopi Culture," *American Anthropologist*, Vol. 47 (1945), pp. 540–553.

3. The belief that one's practical actions have been undertaken in accordance with the beliefs one holds is in no sense limited to the fanatic, although it tends to be most explicitly formulated in such cases. Cf., for example, Eric Hoffer, *The True Believer* (New York: Mentor Books, 1951). For any actor to maintain any claim to act in a principled way, he must be able to see the concordance between his beliefs and practices. If he cannot, it is not a matter of his activity having the character of "being unprincipled," but rather having the character of being senseless—without perceivable pattern. The general problem of the relationship between members' beliefs and their practices and the perception of this relationship to non-members appears to lie at the basis of the conflicting anthropological interpretations of Pueblo Indian life. For an alternative explanation of the

anthropological issue, in terms of the values of the anthropologist, see John Bennett, "The Interpretation of Pueblo Culture: A Question of Values," *Southwestern Journal of Anthropology,* Vol. 2 (1946), pp. 361–374.

4. Cf. Thomas Scheff, "Toward a Sociological Model of Consensus," *American Sociological Review,* Vol. 32 (1967), pp. 32–46.

5. Cf. for example, Ludwig Wittgenstein, *Philosophical Investigation* (New York: The Macmillan Co., 1958), p. 225, on the lack of dispute among mathematicians over the result of a calculation. What Wittgenstein seems to be suggesting here is that, given an agreement among mathematicians covering what "is" and how "what is" is to be manipulated, the conclusions of such manipulations are clearly correct to all concerned.

This characterization of the "impenetrable world view" has been noted for various "deviant" groups. Cf. Egon Bittner, *op. cit.,* and John Lofland, *Doomsday Cult* (Englewood Cliffs, N.J.: Prentice-Hall, 1966).

However, it would seem that the general principles would be applicable regardless of whether the social status of the world view were deviant or conventional. See, for example, Emile Durkheim, *The Elementary Forms of the Religious Life* (Glencoe, Ill.: The Free Press, n.d.), pp. 415–447.

This is not to suggest that members can see no inconsistencies in their belief system itself or in the relationship between their beliefs and their actions. Rather, it is to suggest that what non-members see is likely to cover a range of inconsistent events which is greater than the sub-set of inconsistencies perceivable by members. See, for example, J. L. Simmons, "On Maintaining Deviant Belief Systems," *Social Problems,* Vol. II, pp. 250–256 (1964).

6. Other examples can be found in E. E. Evans-Pritchard, "The Nuer Conception of Spirit in its Relation to the Social Order," *American Anthropologist,* Vol. 55 (1953), pp. 201–202; Simmons, *op. cit.,* p. 254; and Gary Schwartz and Don Merton, "The Language of Adolescents," *A.J.S.,* (1967) LXXII, pp. 453–468.

7. Cf. Alfred Schutz, *Collected Papers,* Vol. 1 (The Hague: Martinius Nijhoff, 1962), pp. 27–47.

8. Such "commonsense" may be alternatively thought of as members expecting candidate members to be able to demonstrate their capacity for what Herbert Simon has called "bounded rationality"—

the capacity to act with respect to the group's typifications. Cf. *Models of Man* (New York: John Wiley and Sons, 1957), p. 198. The nature of this model is that it would be adequate to satisfy the diversity of options, consequences, purposes, and demands characterizing the actual situation. (See also Schutz, *op. cit.*)

# AUTHOR INDEX

# SUBJECT INDEX